CONTENTS

KT-238-422

Chapter 1

A GRAND VOYAGE BEGINS!

On 10 April 1912, the giant ocean liner *Titanic* floated in the harbour at Southampton. The *Titanic* was the largest ship ever built at that time. It was 53 metres tall and almost 270 metres long.

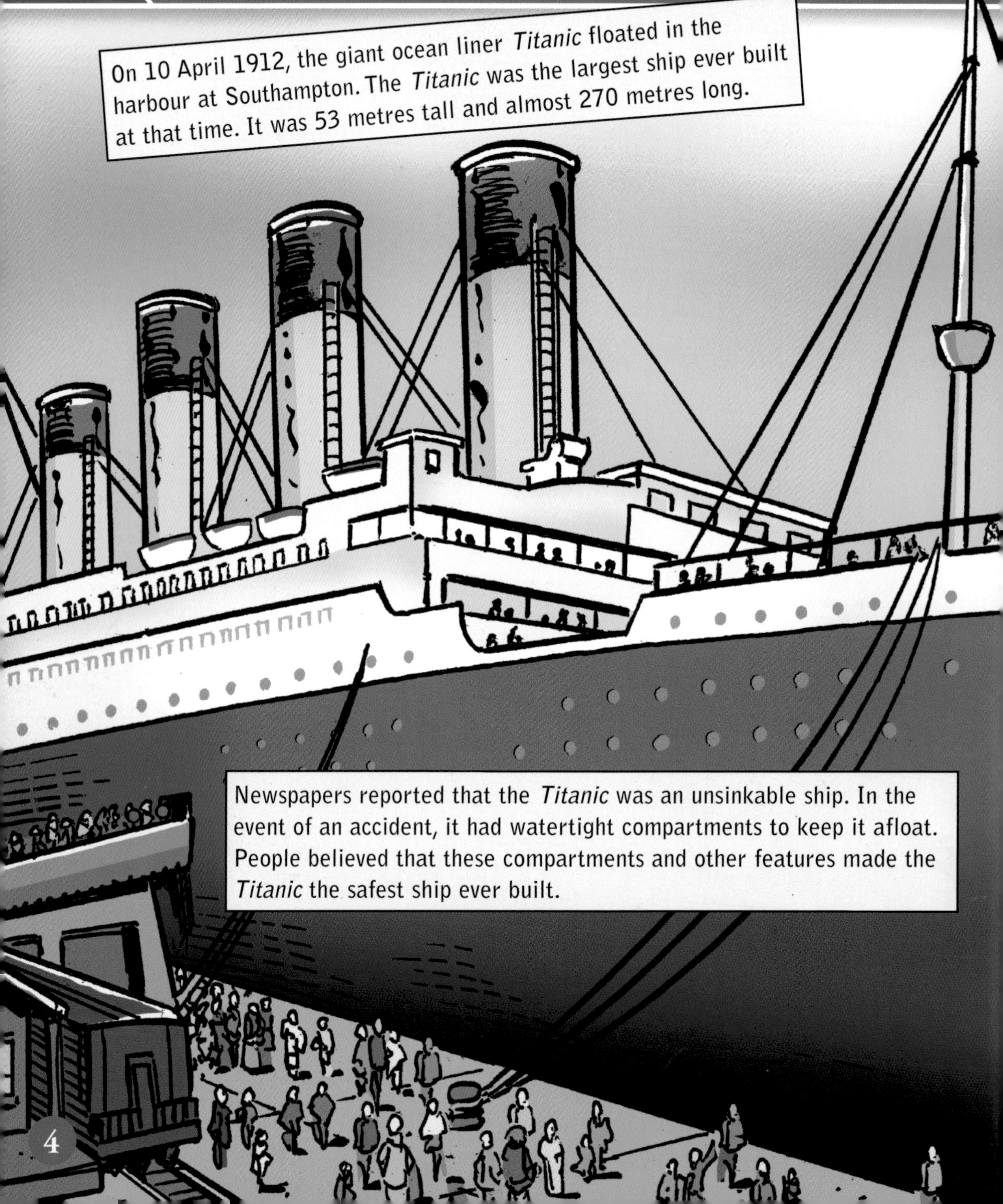

Newspapers reported that the *Titanic* was an unsinkable ship. In the event of an accident, it had watertight compartments to keep it afloat. People believed that these compartments and other features made the *Titanic* the safest ship ever built.

GRAPHIC LIBRARY™

GRAPHIC HISTORY

The Sinking of the TITANIC

by Matt Doeden
illustrated by Charles Barnett
and Phil Miller

Consultant:
Norm Lewis
Canadian Titanic Society
Simcoe, Ontario

Raintree

www.raintreepublishers.co.uk
Visit our website to find out
more information about
Raintree books.

To order:
☎ Phone 0845 6044371
▤ Fax +44 (0) 1865 312263
✉ Email myorders@raintreepublishers.co.uk

Customers from outside the UK please telephone +44 1865 312262

Raintree is an imprint of Capstone Global Library Limited, a company incorporated in England and Wales having its registered
office at 7 Pilgrim Street, London, EC4V 6LB – Registered company number: 6695582

Text © Stone Arch Books 2005
First published in the United Kingdom by Capstone Global Library 2010
Paperback edition first published in the United Kingdom by Capstone Global Library in 2011
The moral rights of the proprietor have been asserted.

Art Director: Jason Knudson
Storyboard Artist: Jason Knudson
Colourist: Brent Schoonover
Editor: Sarah L. Schuette
UK Editor: Vaarunika Dharmapala
Originated by Capstone Global Library Ltd
Printed and bound in China by South China Printing Company Ltd

We would like to thank Philip Charles Crawford, Charles Barnett, and Phil Miller for their assistance
in the preparation of this book.

ISBN 978 1 406214 32 1 (hardback)
14 13 12 11 10
10 9 8 7 6 5 4 3 2 1

ISBN 978 1 406214 37 6 (paperback)
15 14 13 12 11
10 9 8 7 6 5 4 3 2 1

British Library Cataloguing in Publication Data
A full catalogue record for this book is available from the British Library.

Disclaimer
All the Internet addresses (URLs) given in this book were valid at the time of going to press. However, due to the dynamic
nature of the Internet, some addresses may have changed, or sites may have changed or ceased to exist since publication.
While the author and publishers regret any inconvenience this may cause readers, no responsibility for any such changes can be
accepted by either the author or the publishers.

Editor's note: Direct quotations from primary sources are indicated by a yellow background.

Direct quotations appear on the following pages:

Pages 11, 13, 15, 17, 18, 21, 26, from the American and British Titanic Inquiry transcripts (http://www.titanicinquiry.org)

Page 7, from a letter sent before the sinking (http://www.titanic-titanic.com)

Pages 9, 16, from the Marconi Corporation, Ice Warning Messages to and from Titanic
(http://www.marconicalling.com)

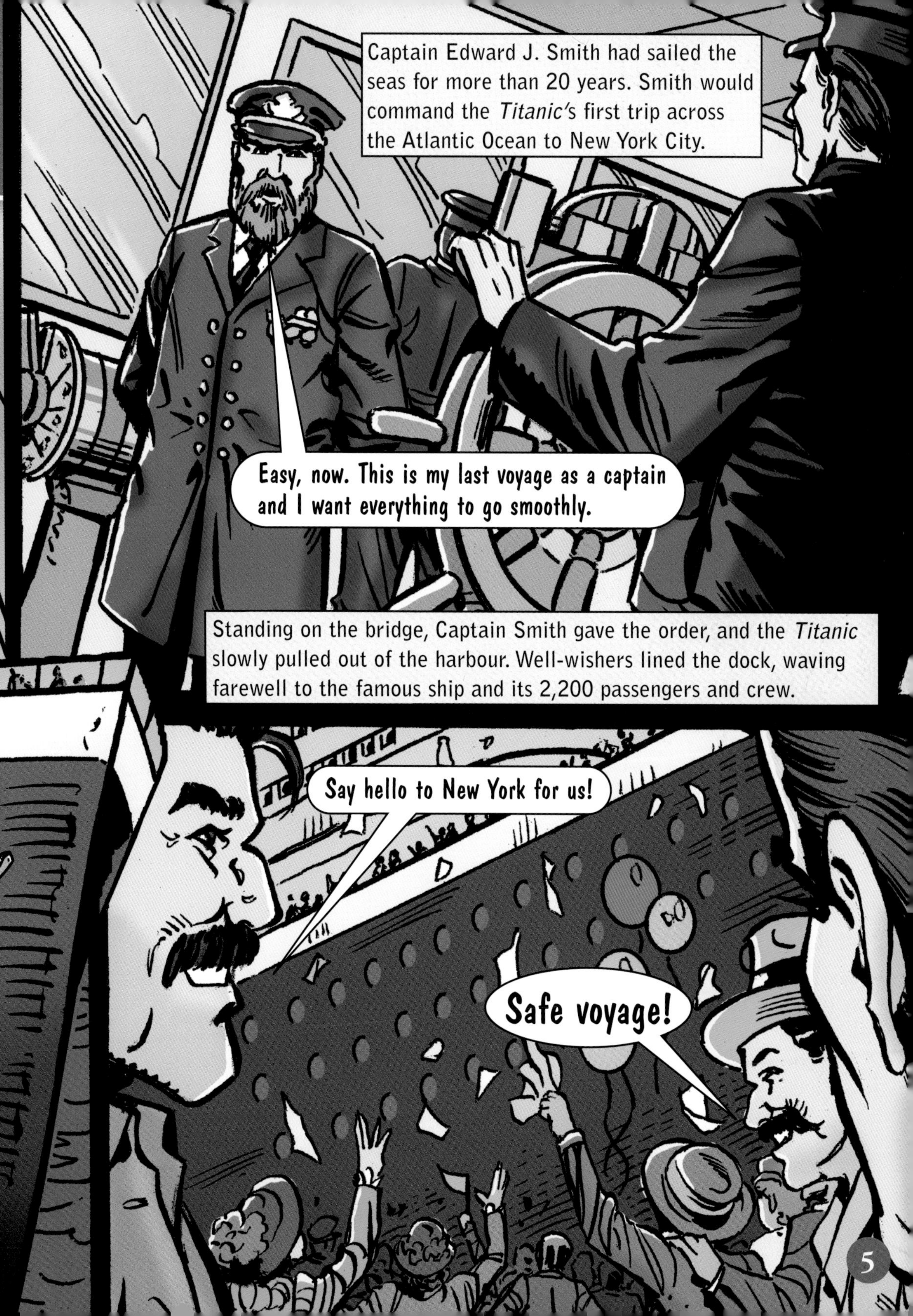
Captain Edward J. Smith had sailed the seas for more than 20 years. Smith would command the *Titanic's* first trip across the Atlantic Ocean to New York City.
Easy, now. This is my last voyage as a captain and I want everything to go smoothly.
Standing on the bridge, Captain Smith gave the order, and the *Titanic* slowly pulled out of the harbour. Well-wishers lined the dock, waving farewell to the famous ship and its 2,200 passengers and crew.
Say hello to New York for us!
Safe voyage!

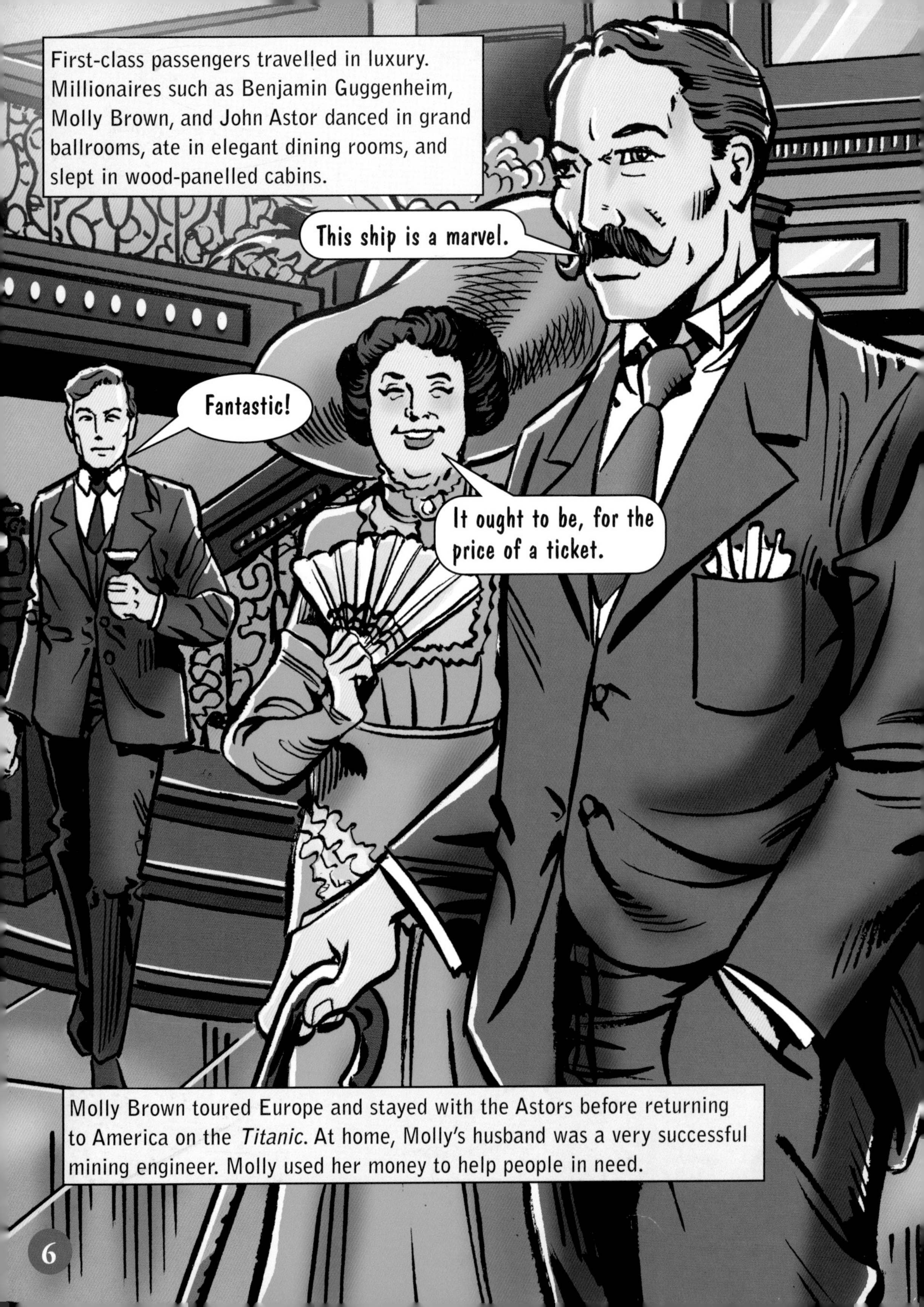
First-class passengers travelled in luxury. Millionaires such as Benjamin Guggenheim, Molly Brown, and John Astor danced in grand ballrooms, ate in elegant dining rooms, and slept in wood-panelled cabins.
This ship is a marvel.
Fantastic!
It ought to be, for the price of a ticket.
Molly Brown toured Europe and stayed with the Astors before returning to America on the *Titanic*. At home, Molly's husband was a very successful mining engineer. Molly used her money to help people in need.

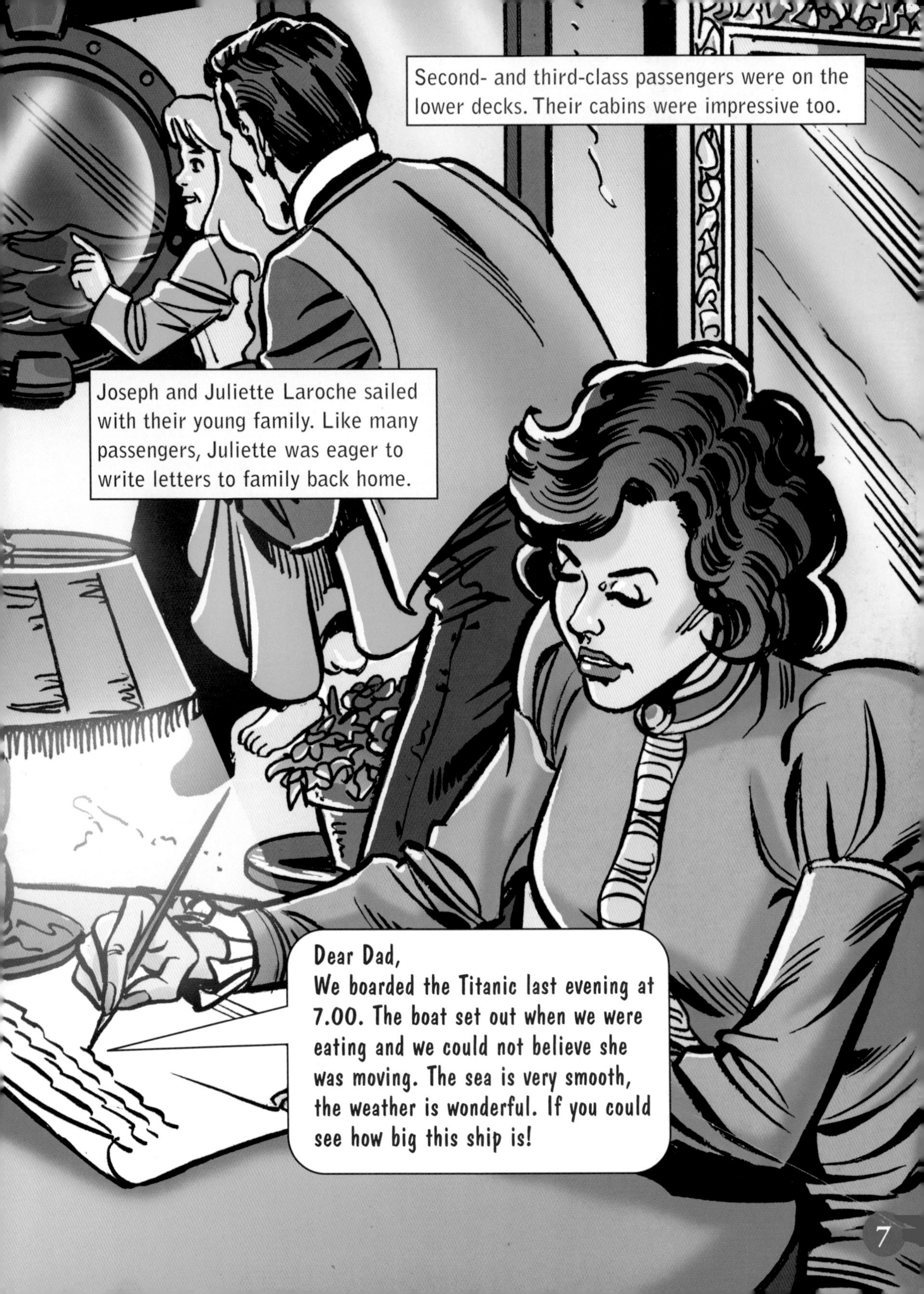
Second- and third-class passengers were on the lower decks. Their cabins were impressive too.
Joseph and Juliette Laroche sailed with their young family. Like many passengers, Juliette was eager to write letters to family back home.
Dear Dad, We boarded the Titanic last evening at 7.00. The boat set out when we were eating and we could not believe she was moving. The sea is very smooth, the weather is wonderful. If you could see how big this ship is!

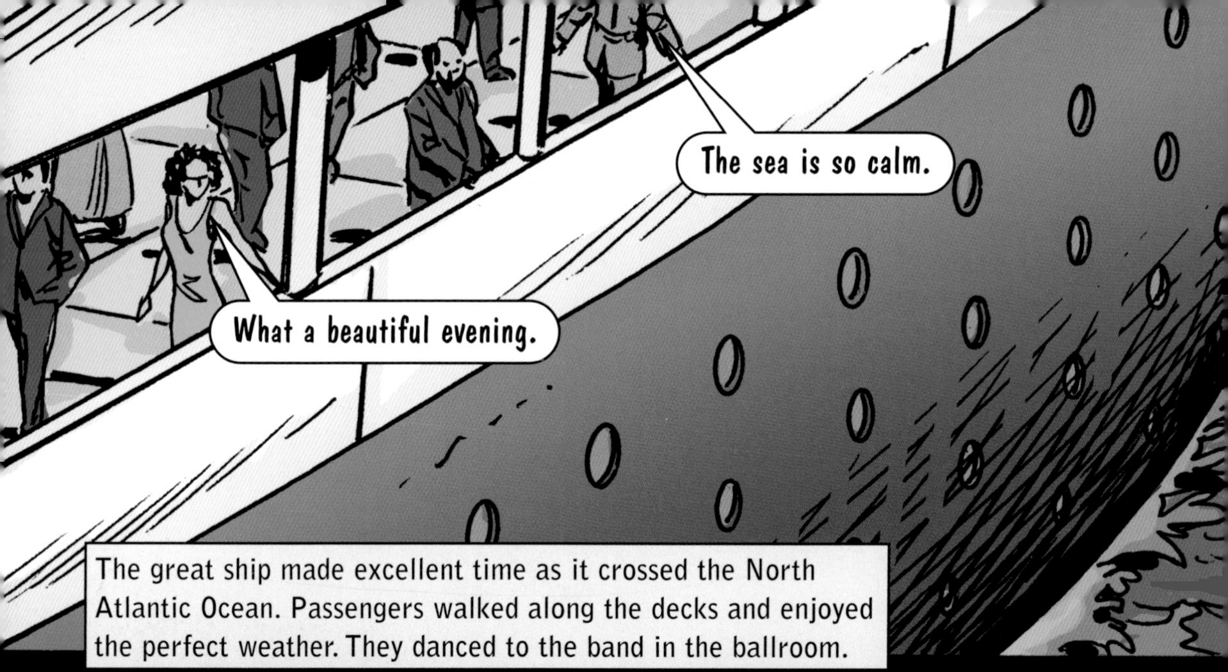
The sea is so calm.
What a beautiful evening.
The great ship made excellent time as it crossed the North Atlantic Ocean. Passengers walked along the decks and enjoyed the perfect weather. They danced to the band in the ballroom.

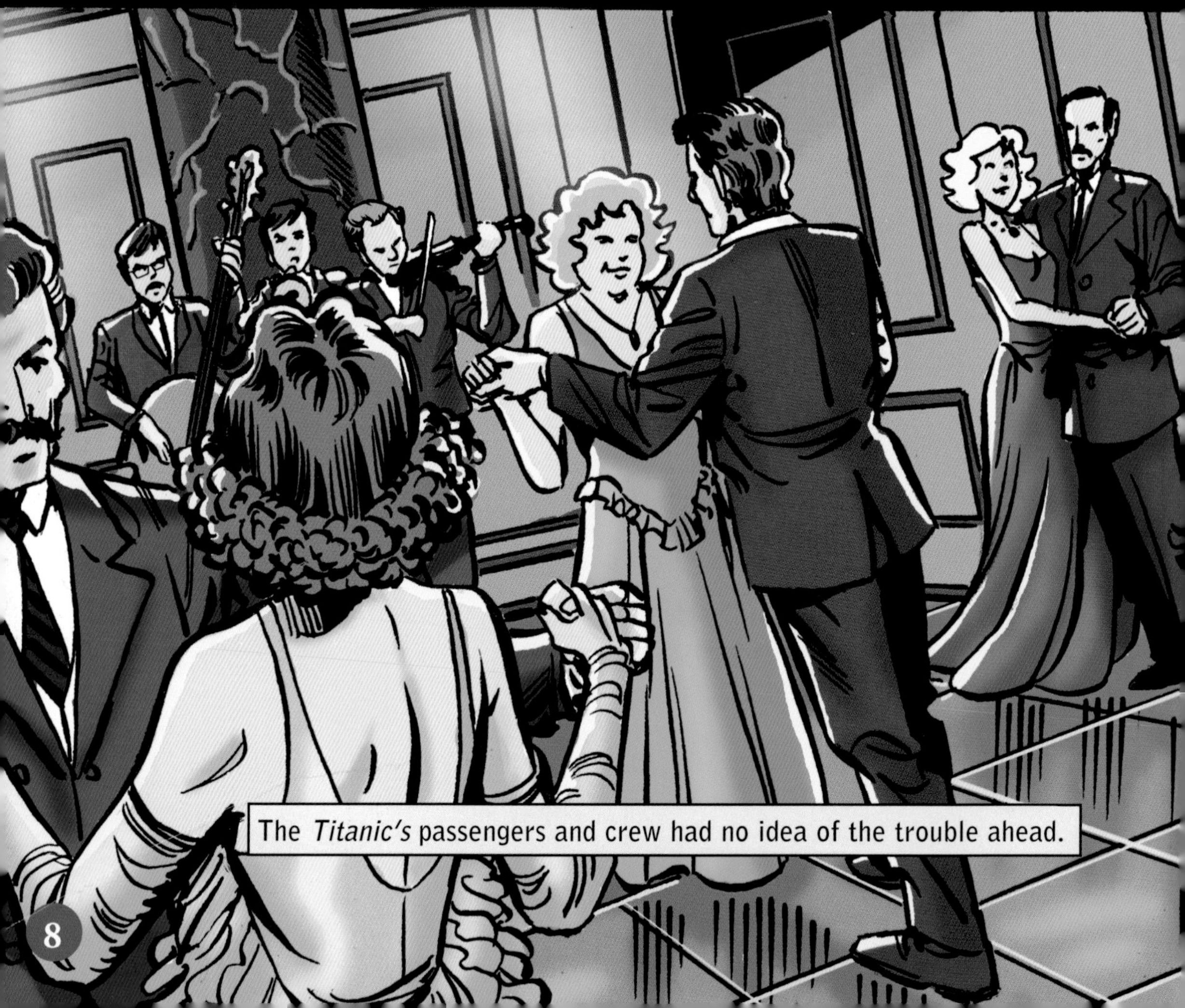
The *Titanic's* passengers and crew had no idea of the trouble ahead.

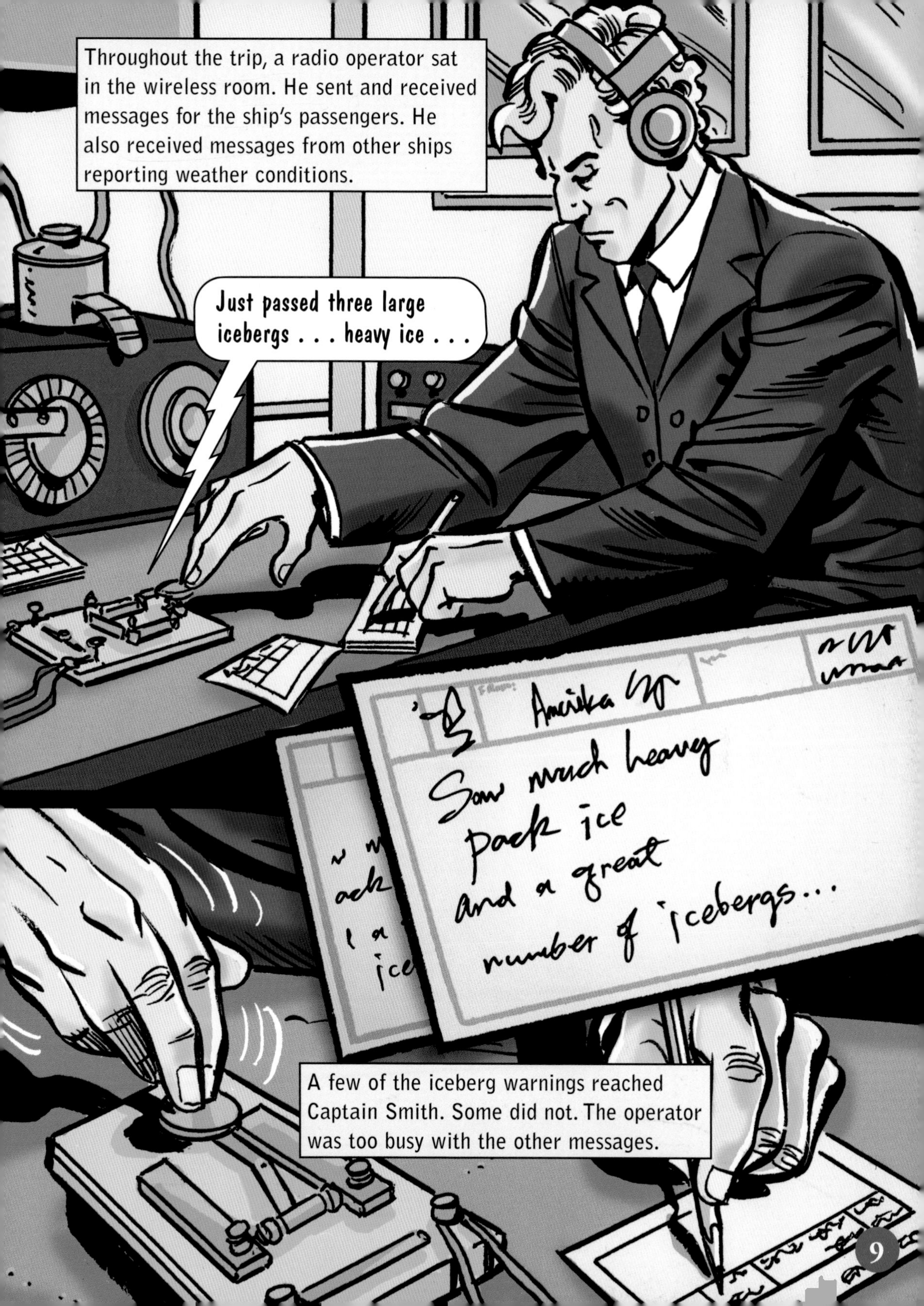
Throughout the trip, a radio operator sat in the wireless room. He sent and received messages for the ship's passengers. He also received messages from other ships reporting weather conditions.
Just passed three large icebergs . . . heavy ice . . .
Amerika
Saw much heavy pack ice and a great number of icebergs...
A few of the iceberg warnings reached Captain Smith. Some did not. The operator was too busy with the other messages.

Chapter 2

COLLISION

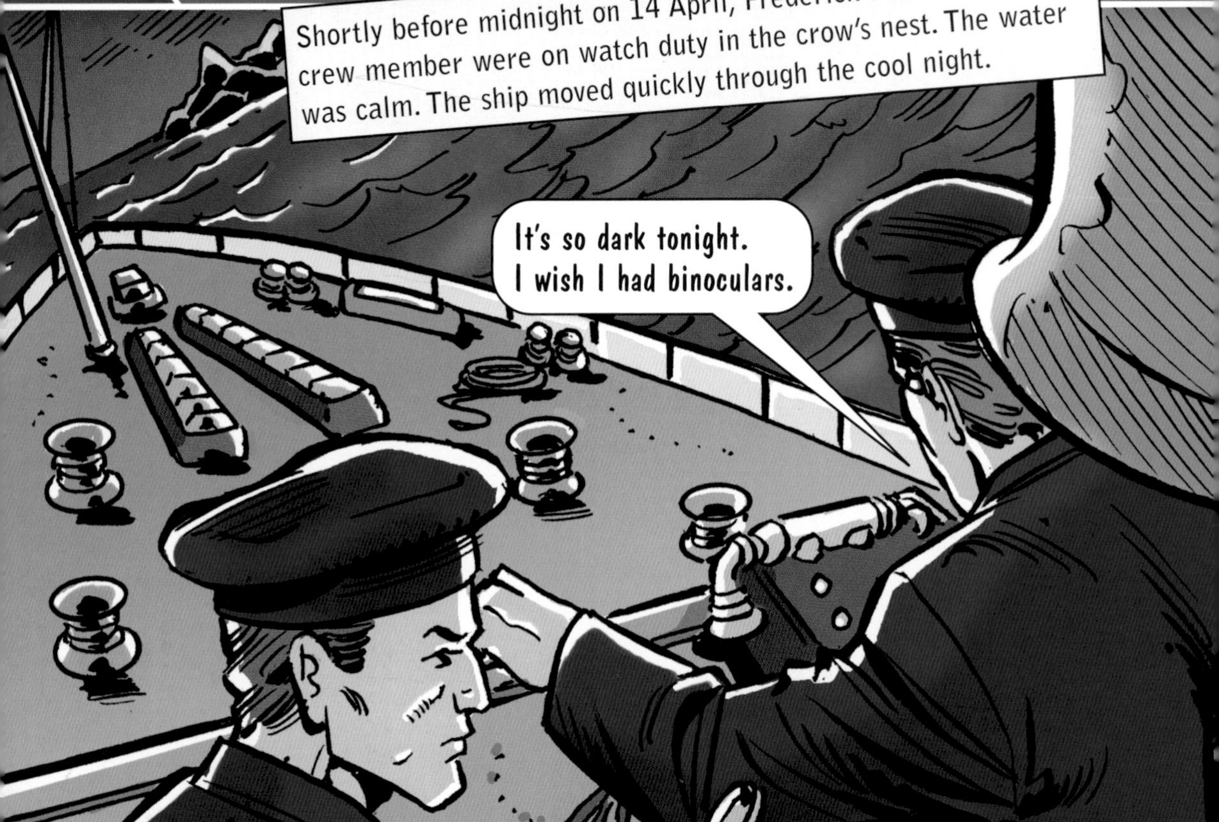
Shortly before midnight on 14 April, Frederick Fleet and another crew member were on watch duty in the crow's nest. The water was calm. The ship moved quickly through the cool night.
It's so dark tonight. I wish I had binoculars.

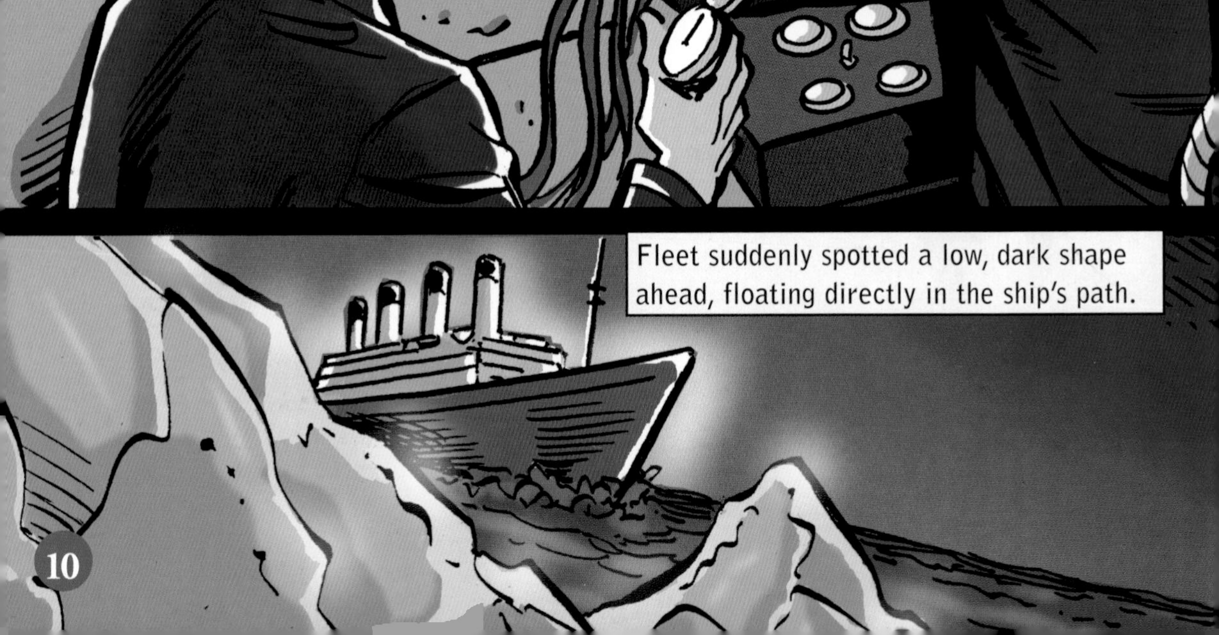
Fleet suddenly spotted a low, dark shape ahead, floating directly in the ship's path.

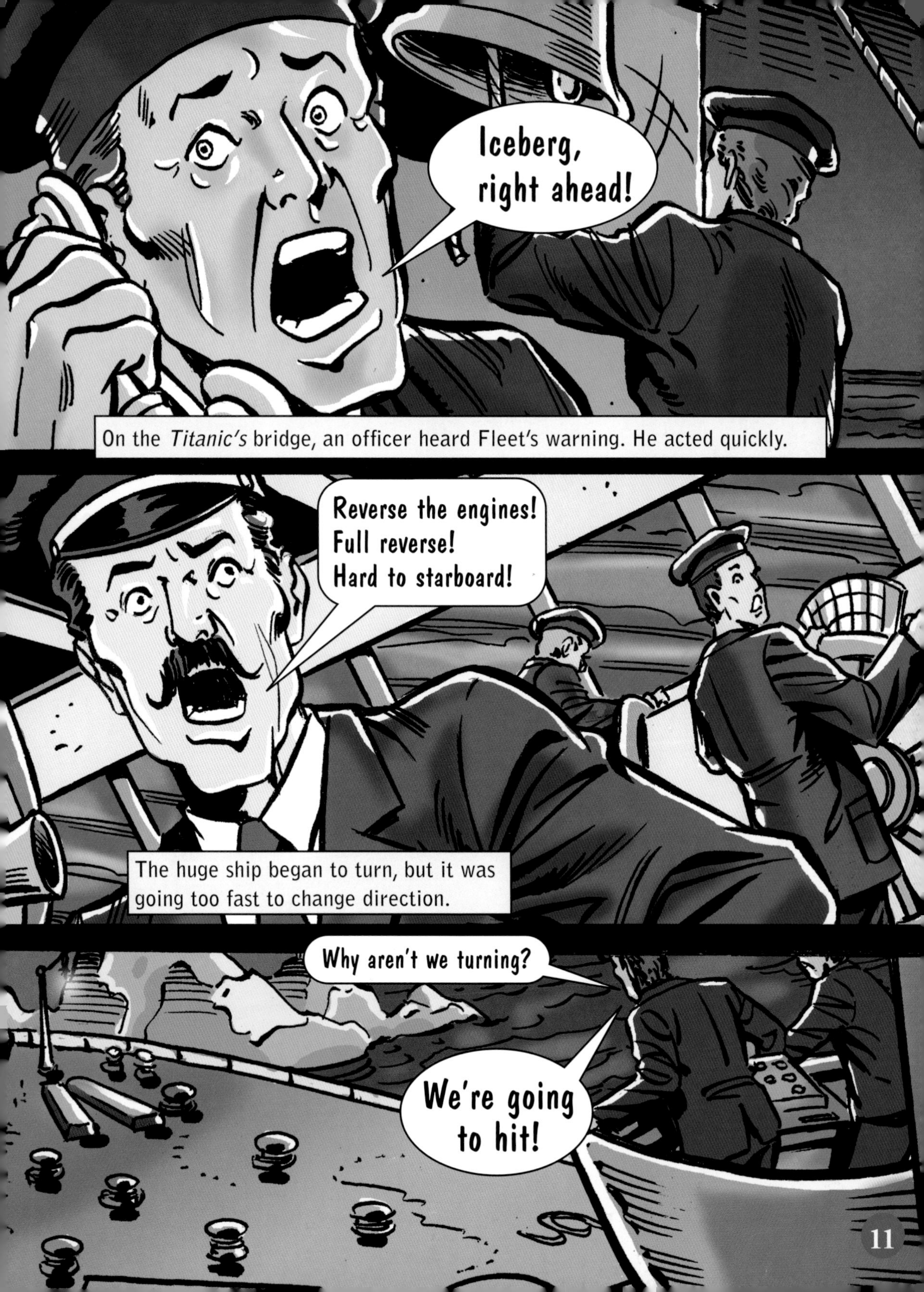
Iceberg, right ahead!
On the *Titanic's* bridge, an officer heard Fleet's warning. He acted quickly.
Reverse the engines! Full reverse! Hard to starboard!
The huge ship began to turn, but it was going too fast to change direction.
Why aren't we turning?
We're going to hit!

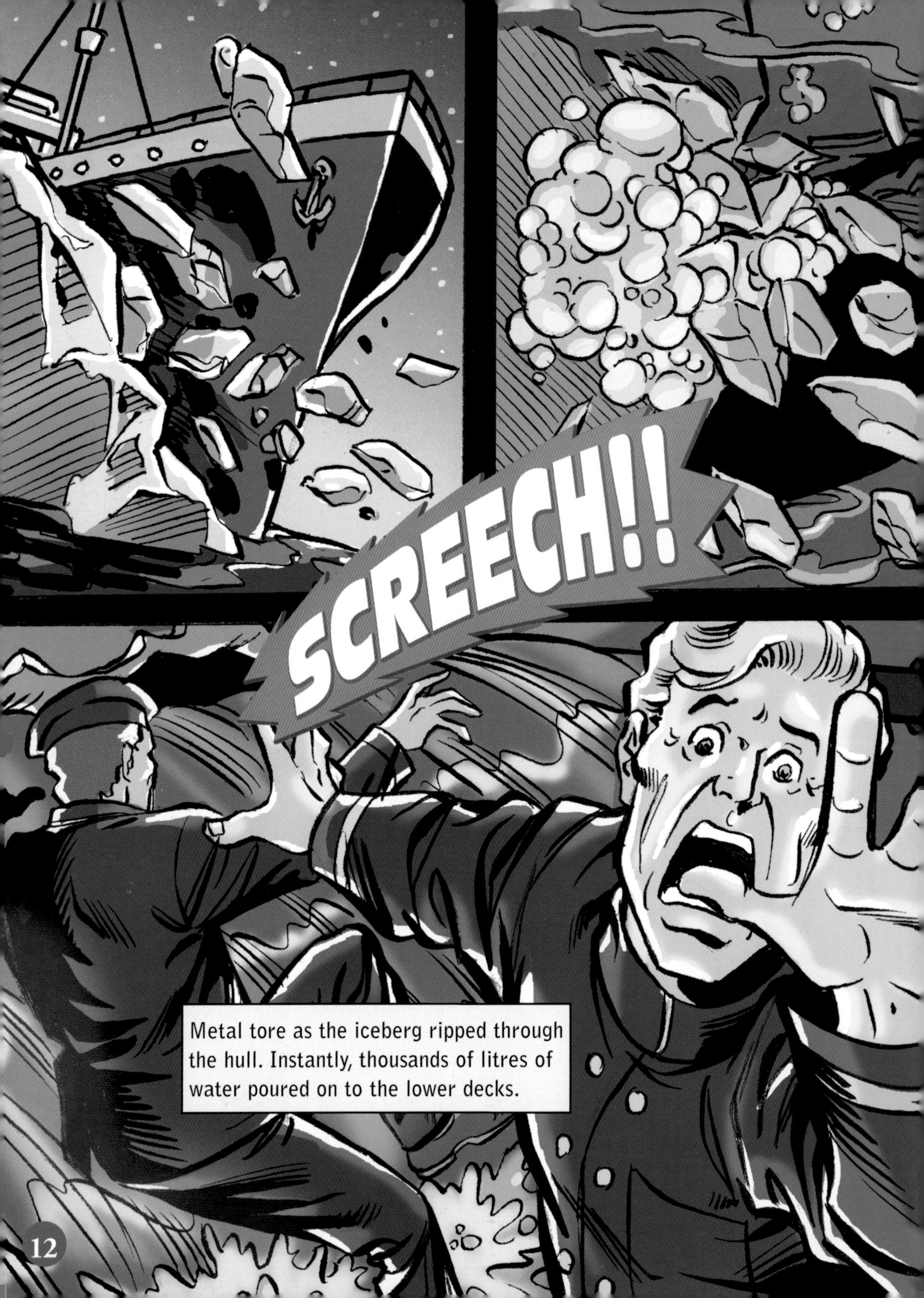
SCREECH!!
Metal tore as the iceberg ripped through the hull. Instantly, thousands of litres of water poured on to the lower decks.

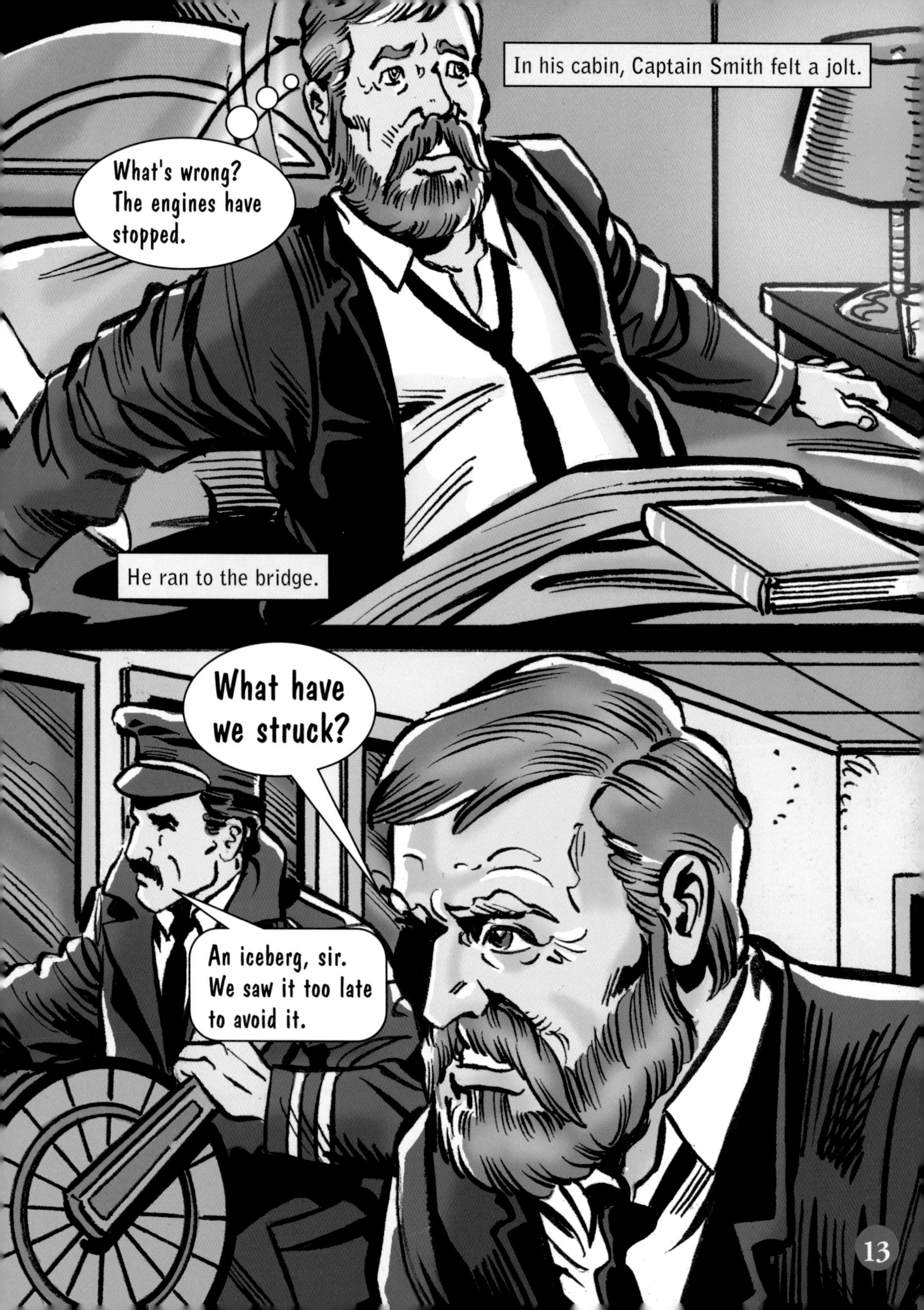
In his cabin, Captain Smith felt a jolt.
What's wrong? The engines have stopped.
He ran to the bridge.
What have we struck?
An iceberg, sir. We saw it too late to avoid it.

Chapter 3

THE *TITANIC*'S FATE IS SEALED

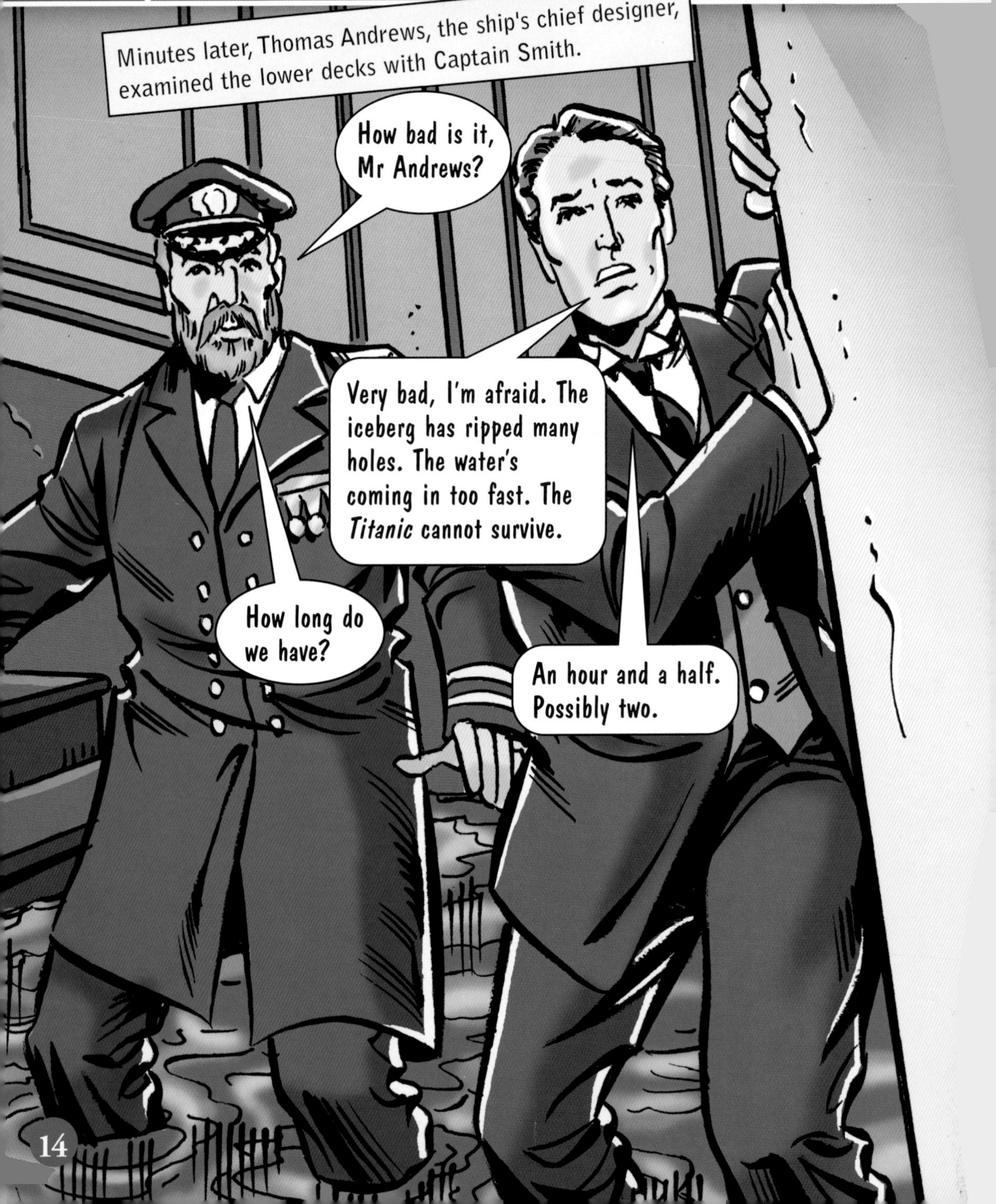
Minutes later, Thomas Andrews, the ship's chief designer, examined the lower decks with Captain Smith.
How bad is it, Mr Andrews?
Very bad, I'm afraid. The iceberg has ripped many holes. The water's coming in too fast. The *Titanic* cannot survive.
How long do we have?
An hour and a half. Possibly two.

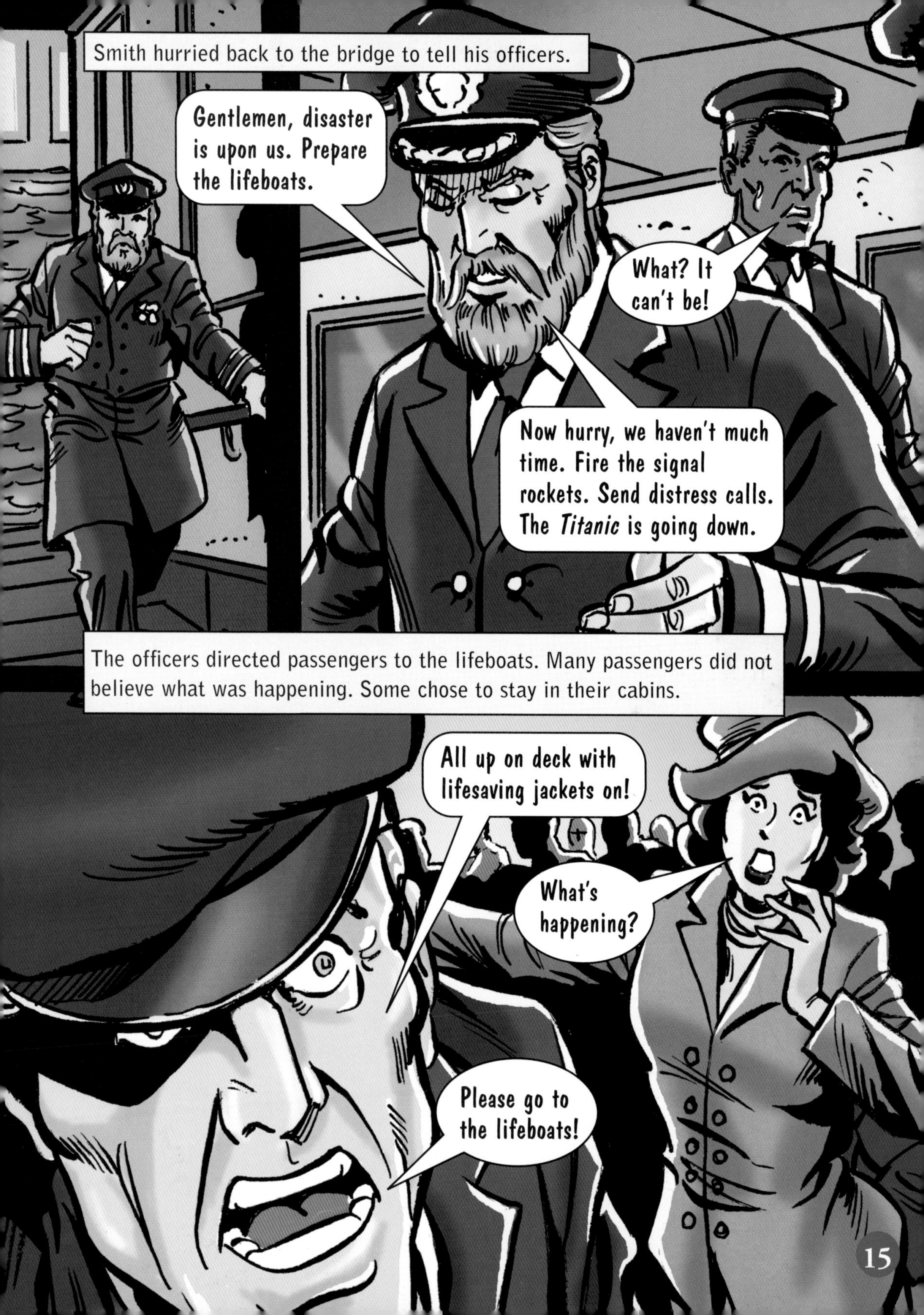
Smith hurried back to the bridge to tell his officers.
Gentlemen, disaster is upon us. Prepare the lifeboats.
What? It can't be!
Now hurry, we haven't much time. Fire the signal rockets. Send distress calls. The *Titanic* is going down.
The officers directed passengers to the lifeboats. Many passengers did not believe what was happening. Some chose to stay in their cabins.
All up on deck with lifesaving jackets on!
What's happening?
Please go to the lifeboats!

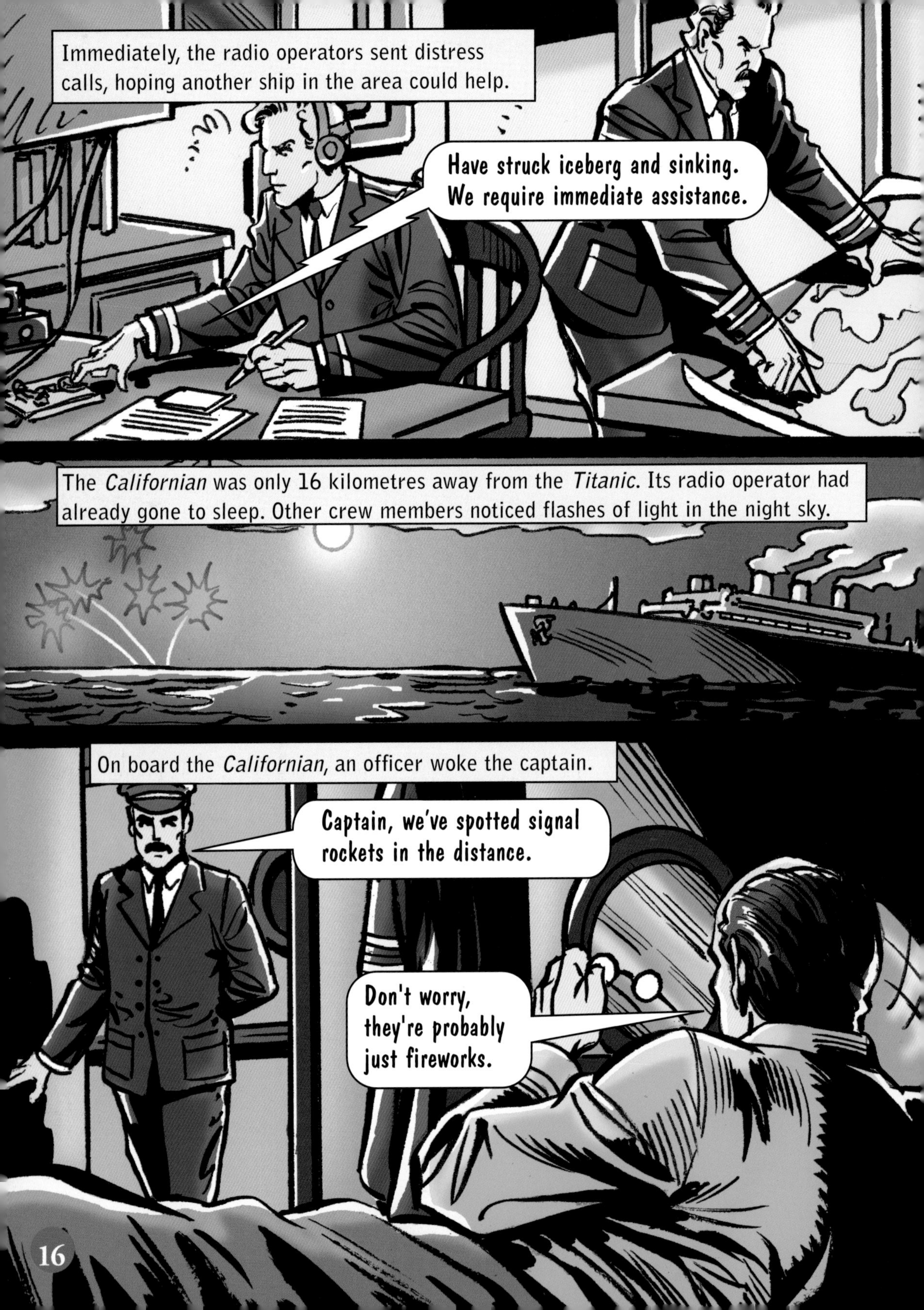
Immediately, the radio operators sent distress calls, hoping another ship in the area could help.
Have struck iceberg and sinking. We require immediate assistance.
The Californian was only 16 kilometres away from the Titanic. Its radio operator had already gone to sleep. Other crew members noticed flashes of light in the night sky.
On board the Californian, an officer woke the captain.
Captain, we've spotted signal rockets in the distance.
Don't worry, they're probably just fireworks.

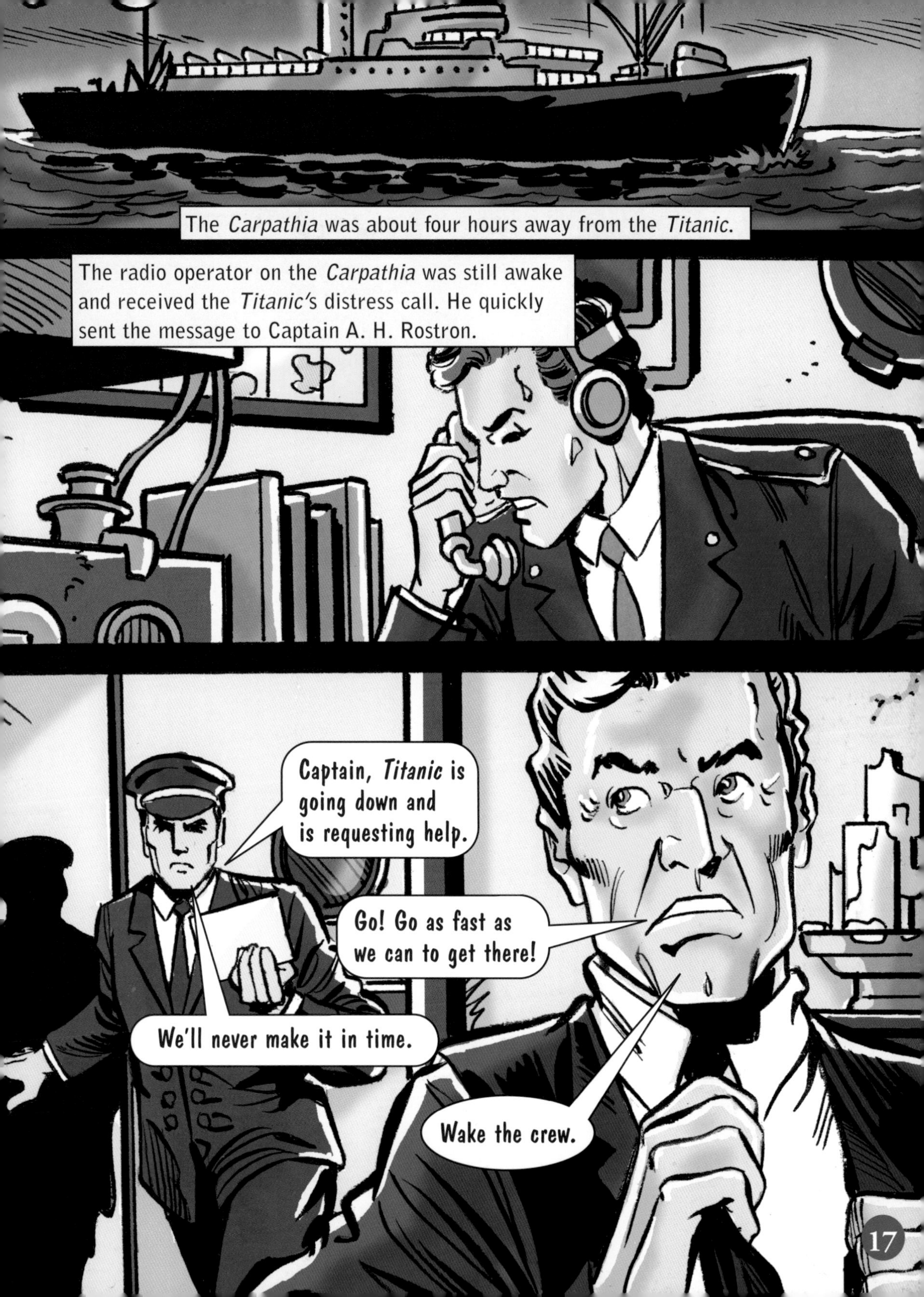
The *Carpathia* was about four hours away from the *Titanic*.
The radio operator on the *Carpathia* was still awake and received the *Titanic*'s distress call. He quickly sent the message to Captain A. H. Rostron.
Captain, *Titanic* is going down and is requesting help.
Go! Go as fast as we can to get there!
We'll never make it in time.
Wake the crew.

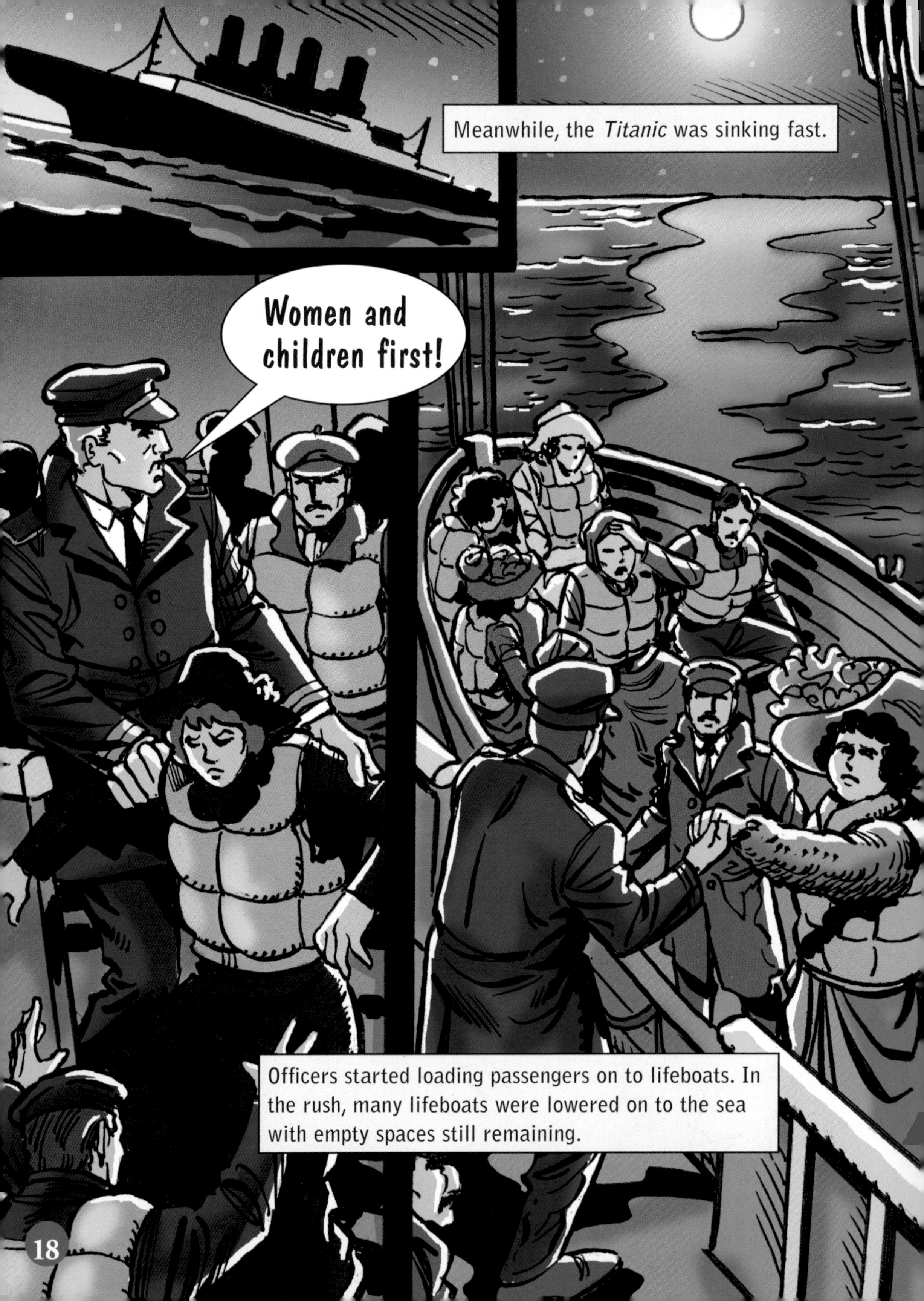

Meanwhile, the *Titanic* was sinking fast.
Women and children first!
Officers started loading passengers on to lifeboats. In the rush, many lifeboats were lowered on to the sea with empty spaces still remaining.

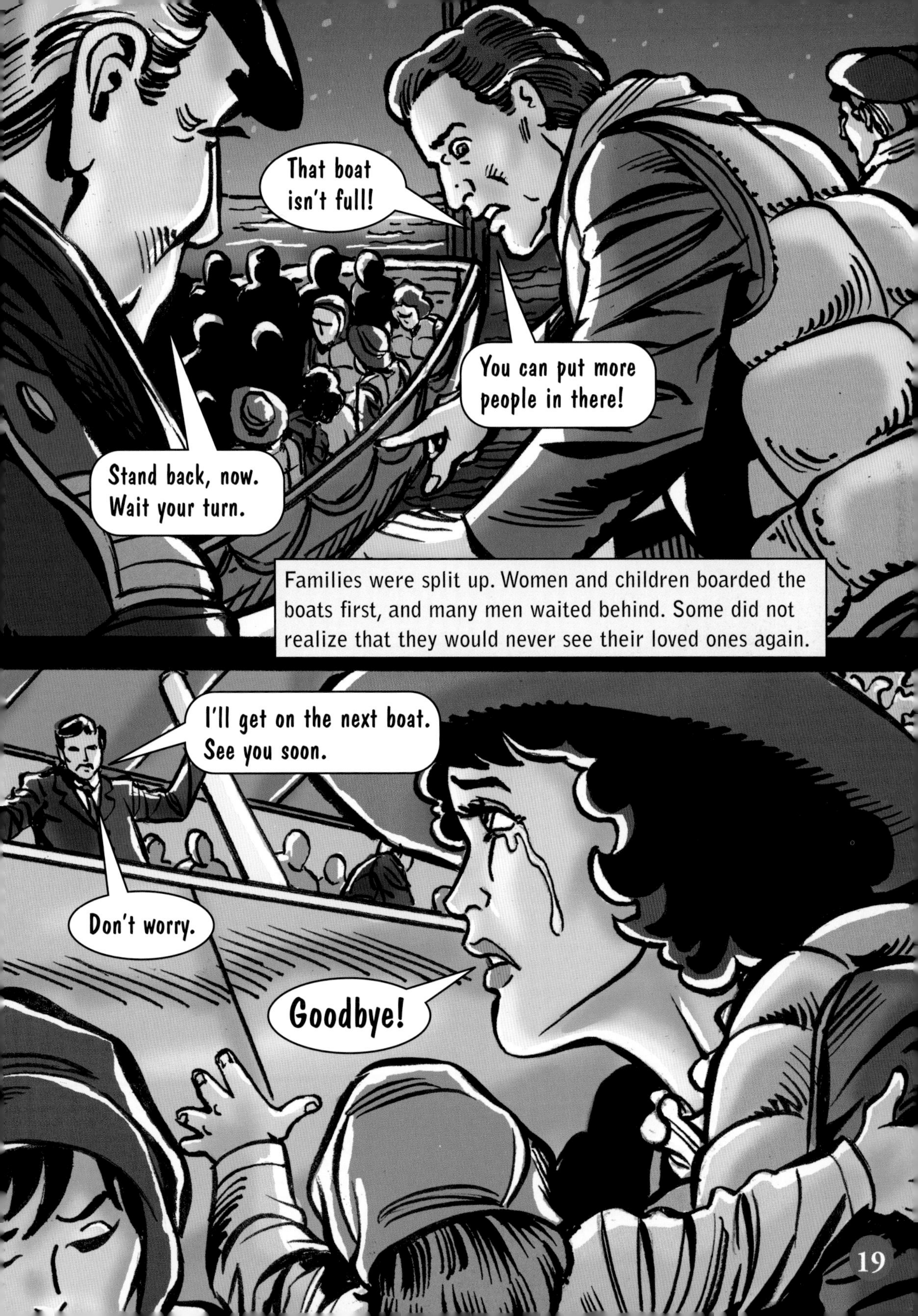
That boat isn't full!
You can put more people in there!
Stand back, now. Wait your turn.
Families were split up. Women and children boarded the boats first, and many men waited behind. Some did not realize that they would never see their loved ones again.
I'll get on the next boat. See you soon.
Don't worry.
Goodbye!

Chapter 4

THE END OF THE *TITANIC*

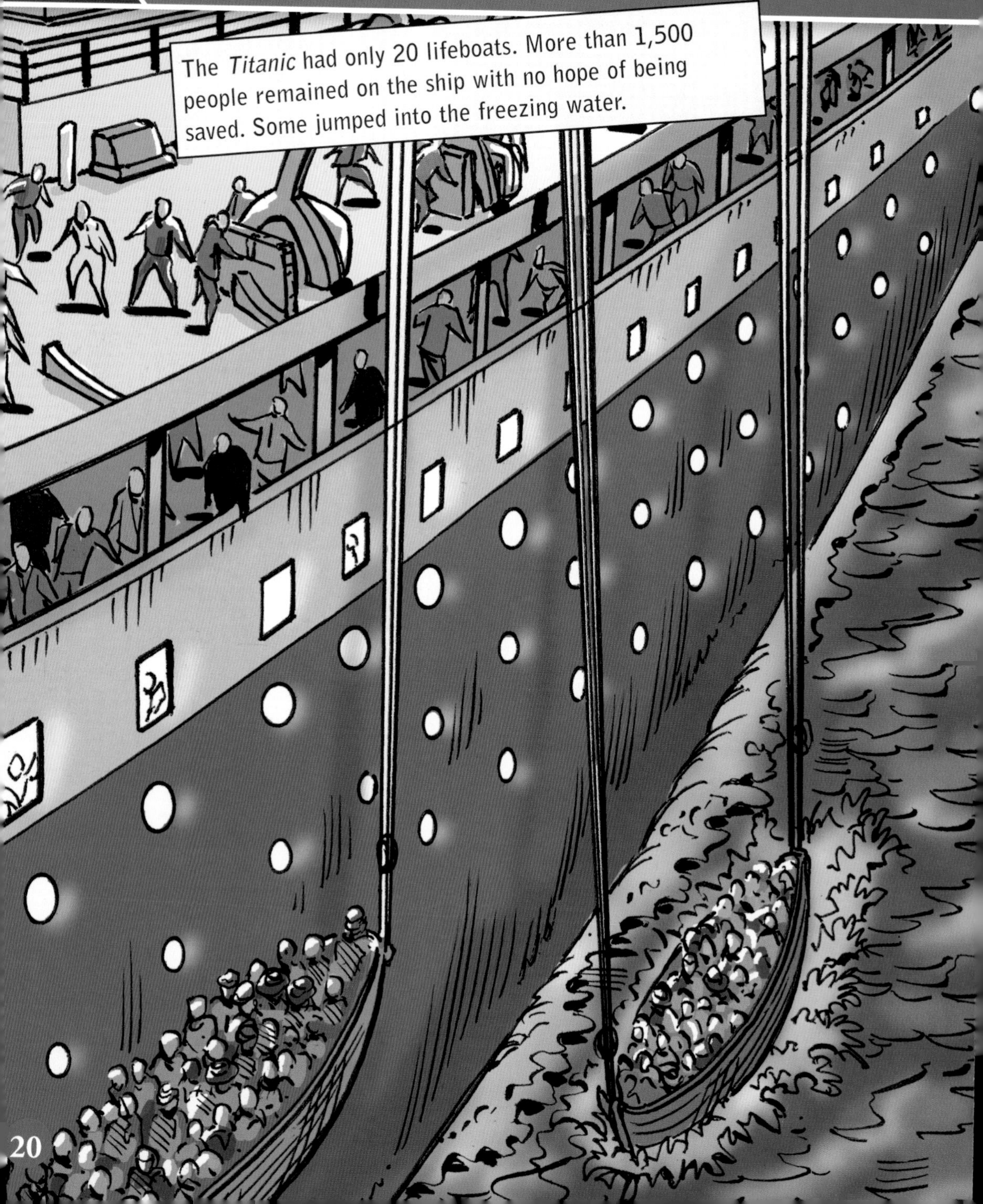
The *Titanic* had only 20 lifeboats. More than 1,500 people remained on the ship with no hope of being saved. Some jumped into the freezing water.

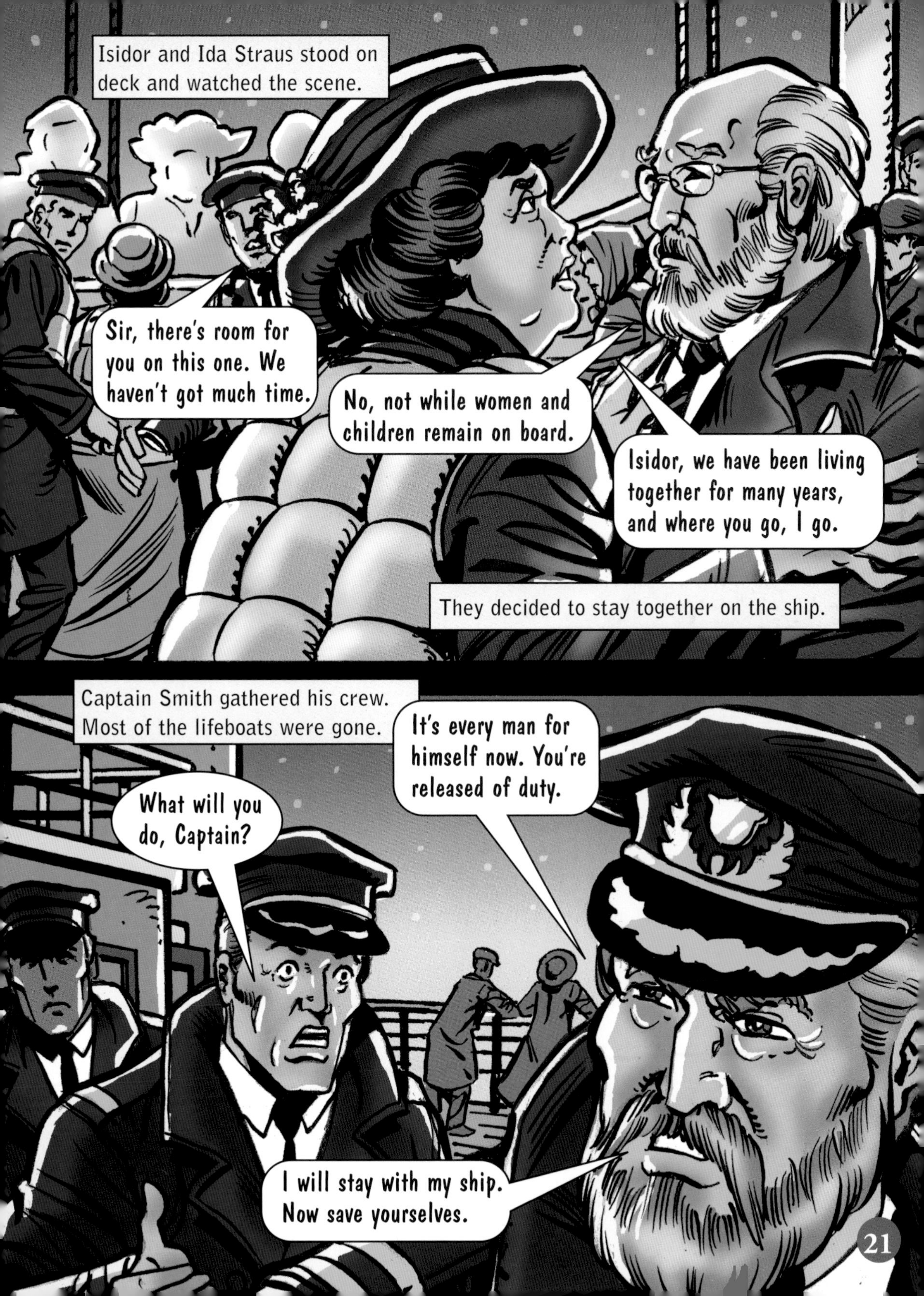
Isidor and Ida Straus stood on deck and watched the scene.
Sir, there's room for you on this one. We haven't got much time.
No, not while women and children remain on board.
Isidor, we have been living together for many years, and where you go, I go.
They decided to stay together on the ship.
Captain Smith gathered his crew. Most of the lifeboats were gone.
It's every man for himself now. You're released of duty.
What will you do, Captain?
I will stay with my ship. Now save yourselves.

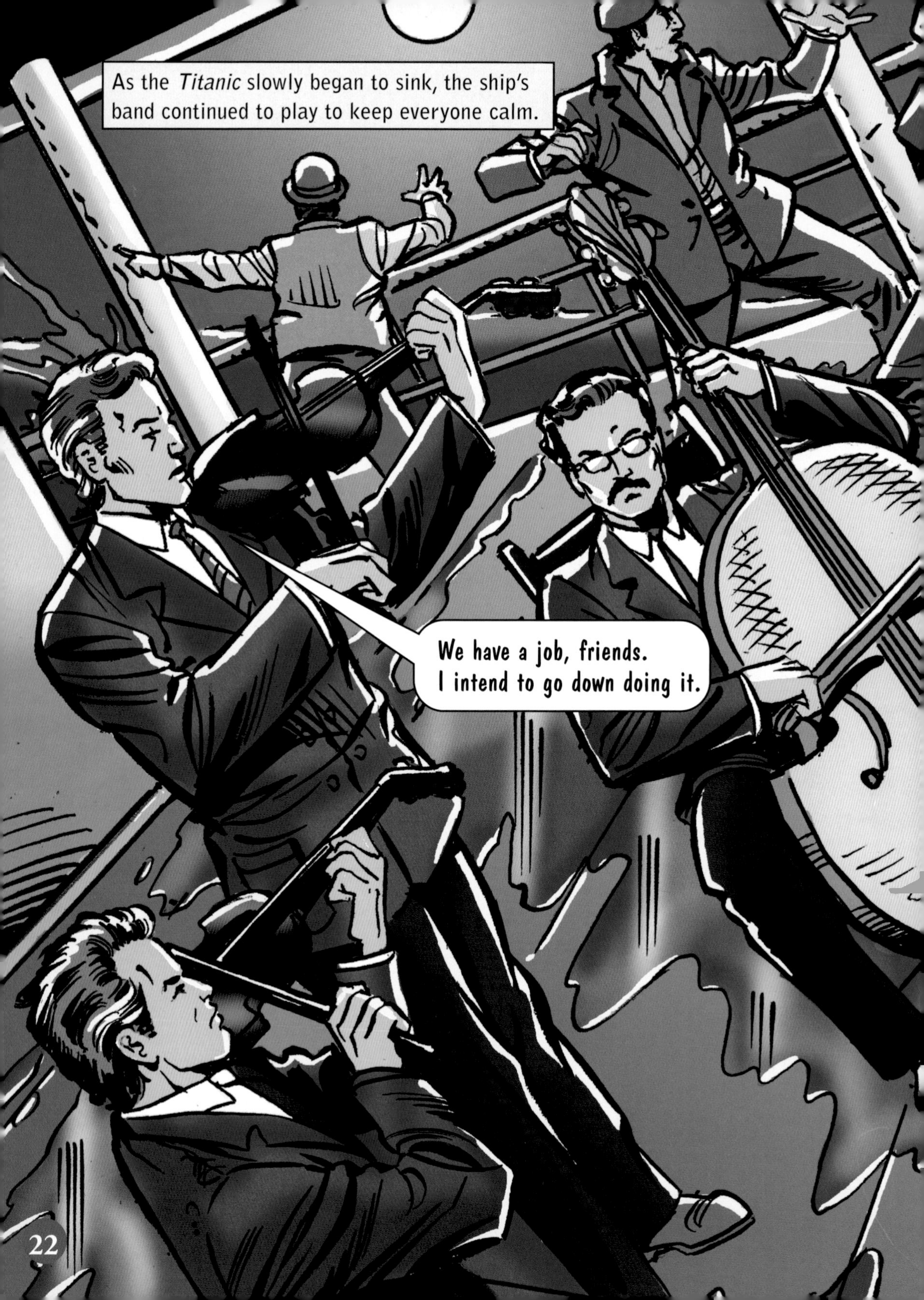
As the *Titanic* slowly began to sink, the ship's band continued to play to keep everyone calm.
We have a job, friends. I intend to go down doing it.

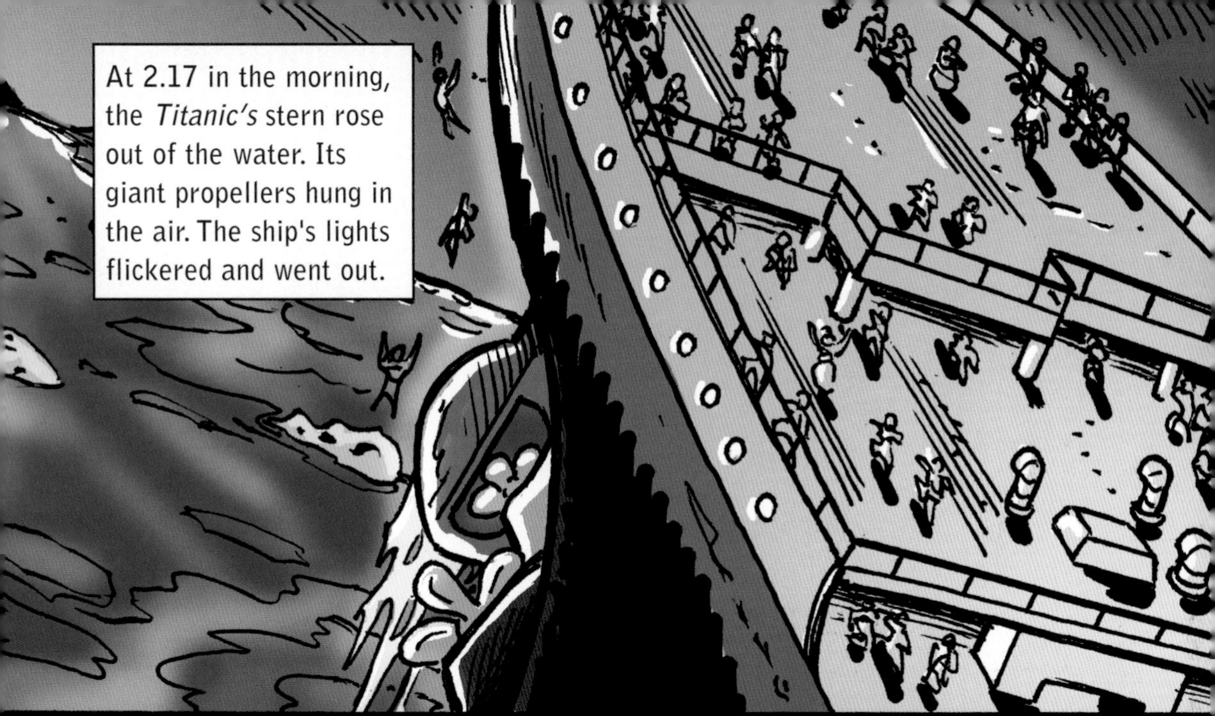
At 2.17 in the morning, the *Titanic's* stern rose out of the water. Its giant propellers hung in the air. The ship's lights flickered and went out.

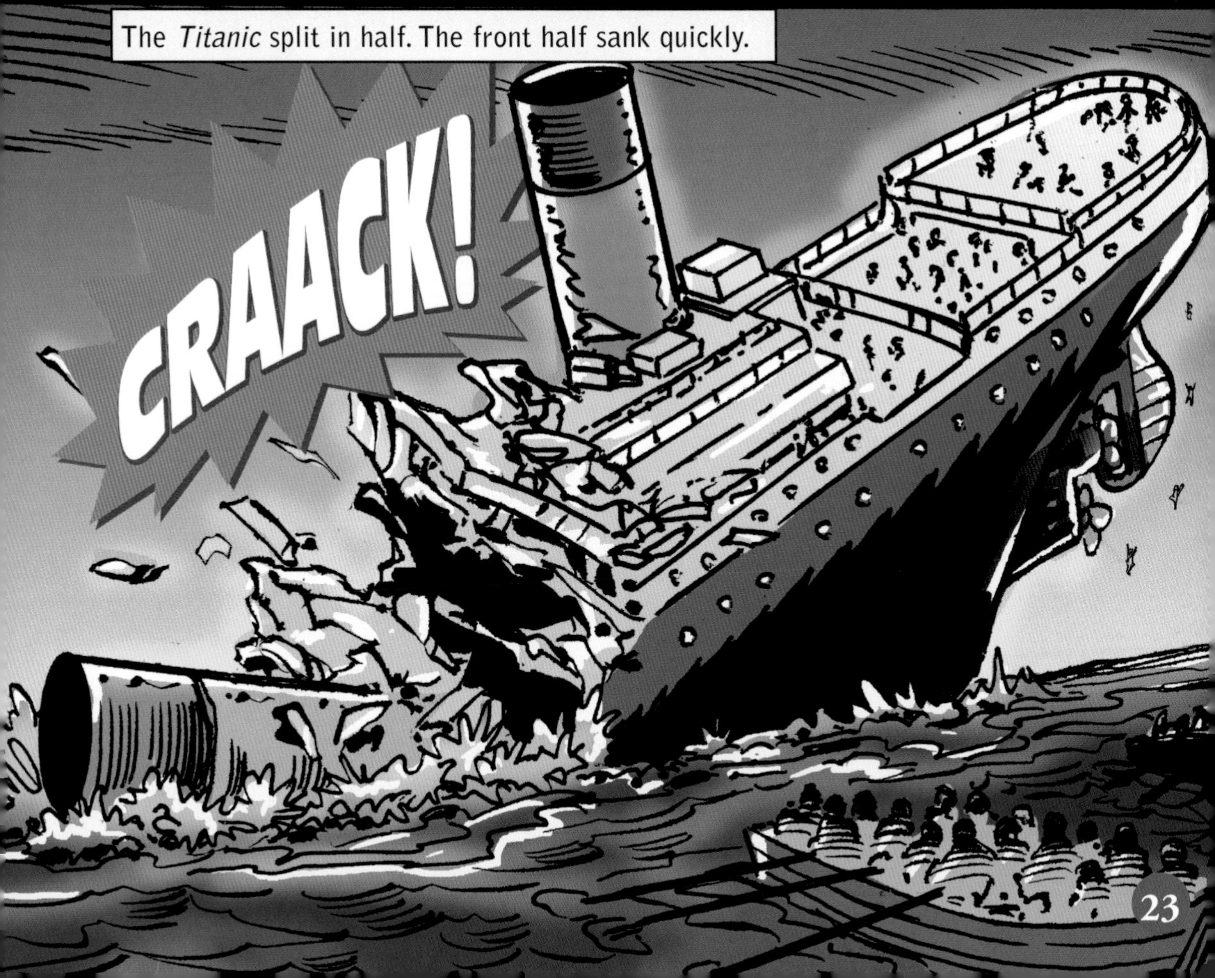
The *Titanic* split in half. The front half sank quickly.
CRAACK!

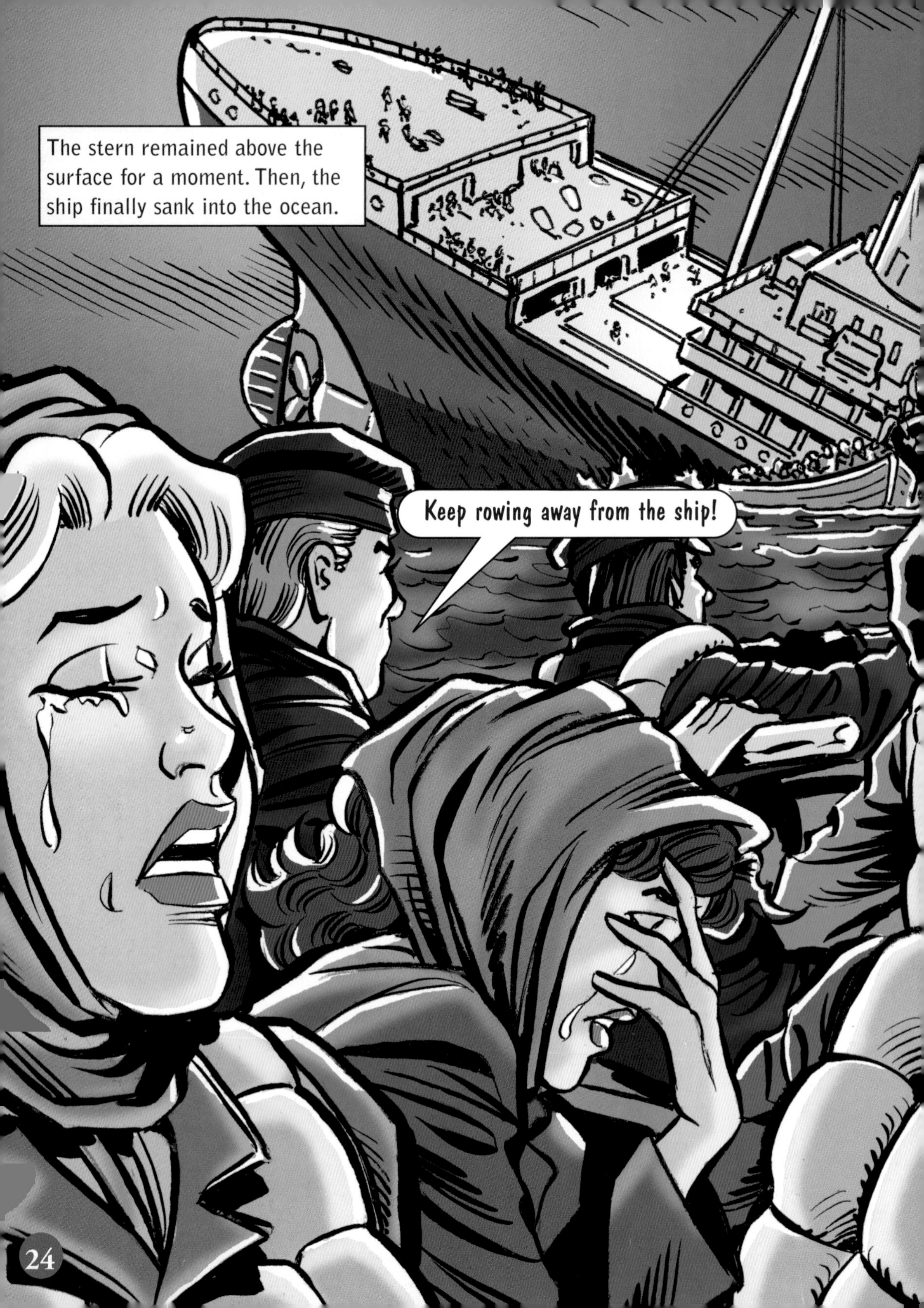
The stern remained above the surface for a moment. Then, the ship finally sank into the ocean.
Keep rowing away from the ship!

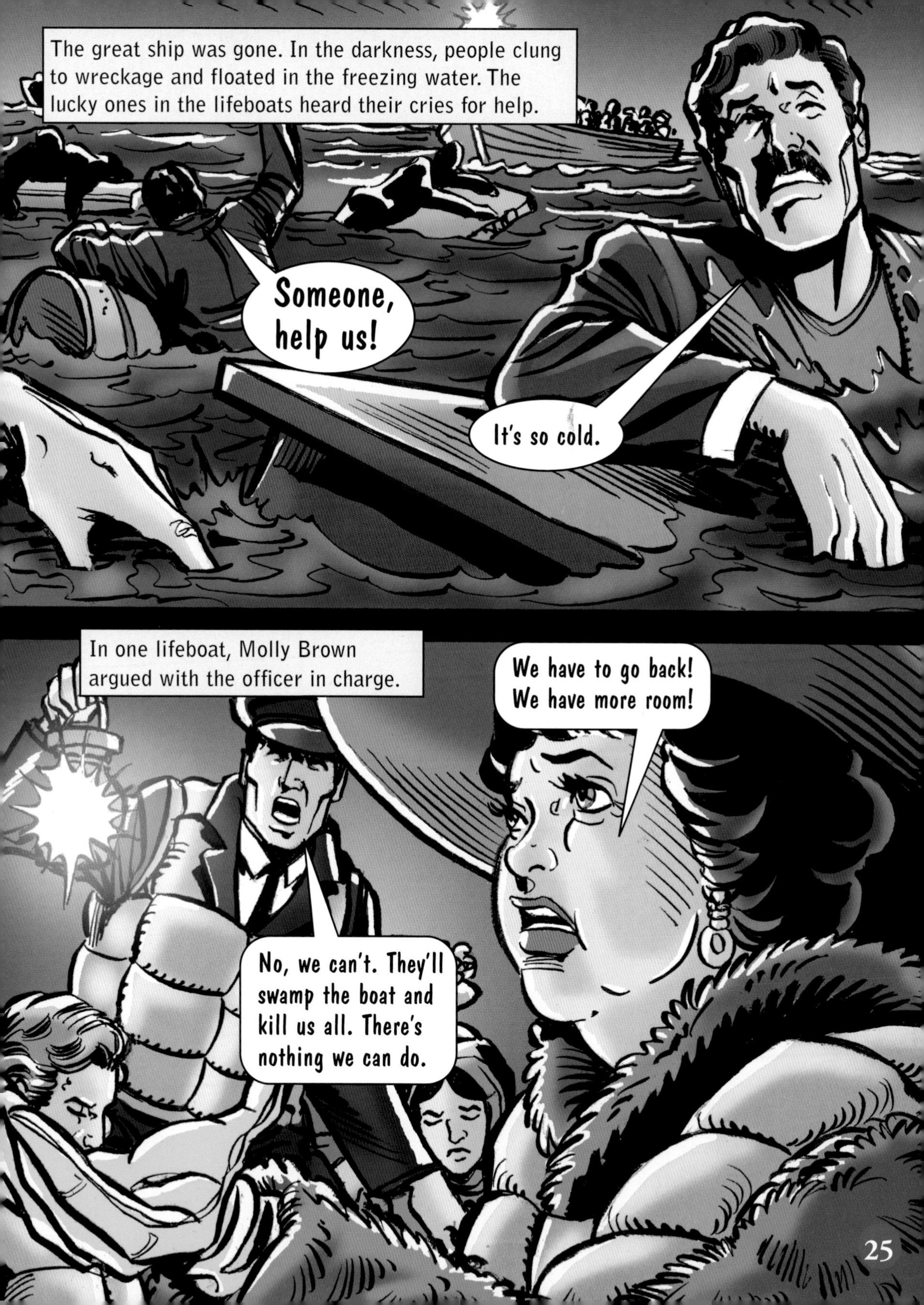
The great ship was gone. In the darkness, people clung to wreckage and floated in the freezing water. The lucky ones in the lifeboats heard their cries for help.
Someone, help us!
It's so cold.
In one lifeboat, Molly Brown argued with the officer in charge.
We have to go back! We have more room!
No, we can't. They'll swamp the boat and kill us all. There's nothing we can do.

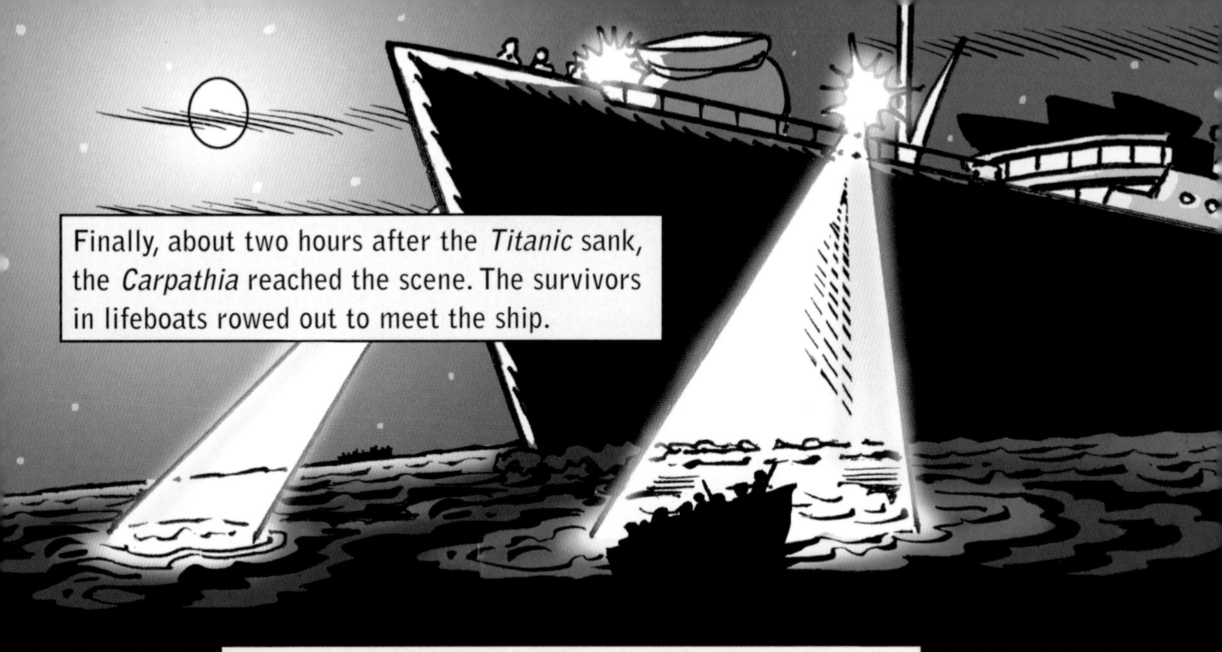
Finally, about two hours after the *Titanic* sank, the *Carpathia* reached the scene. The survivors in lifeboats rowed out to meet the ship.

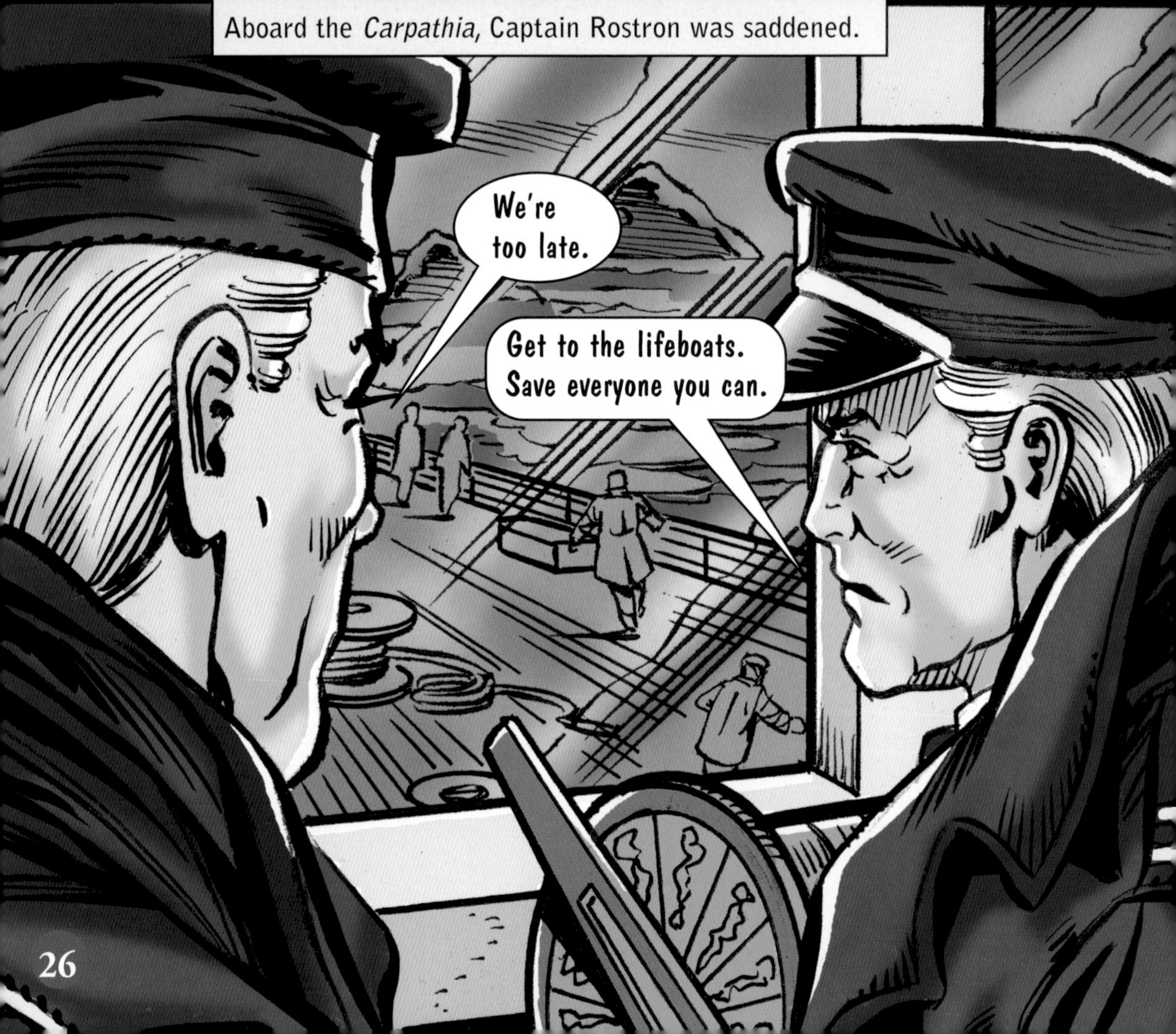
Aboard the *Carpathia*, Captain Rostron was saddened.
We're too late.
Get to the lifeboats. Save everyone you can.

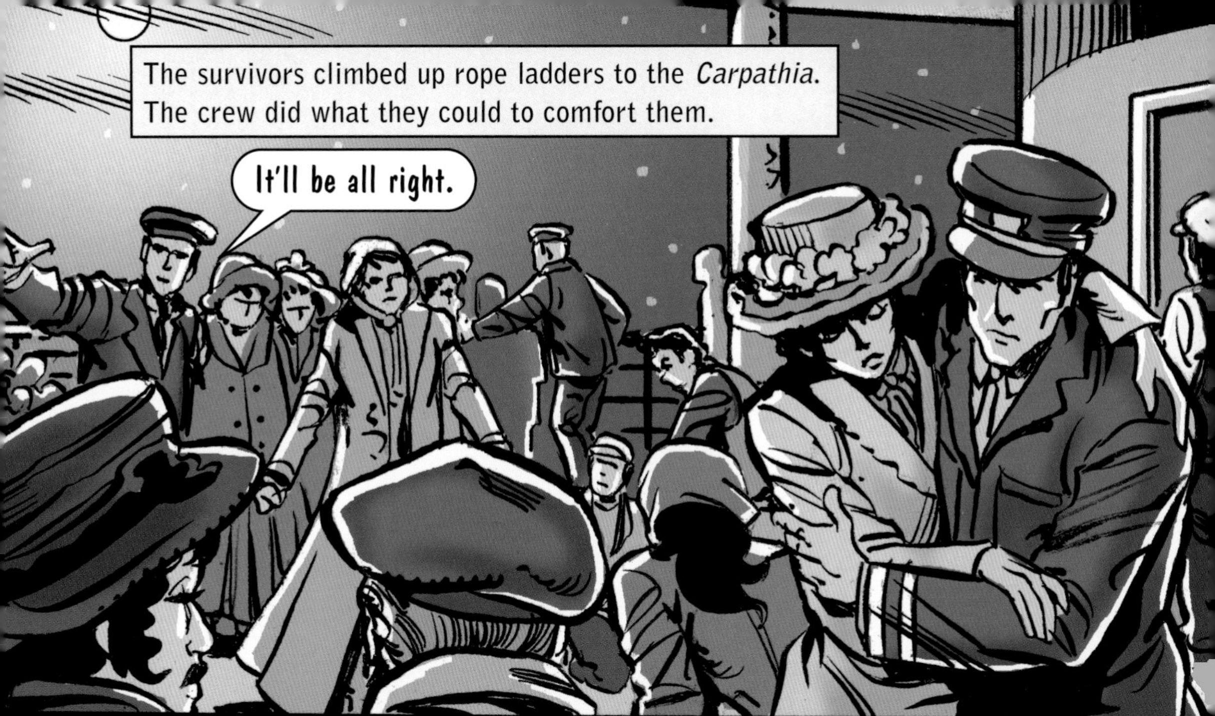
The survivors climbed up rope ladders to the *Carpathia*. The crew did what they could to comfort them.
It'll be all right.

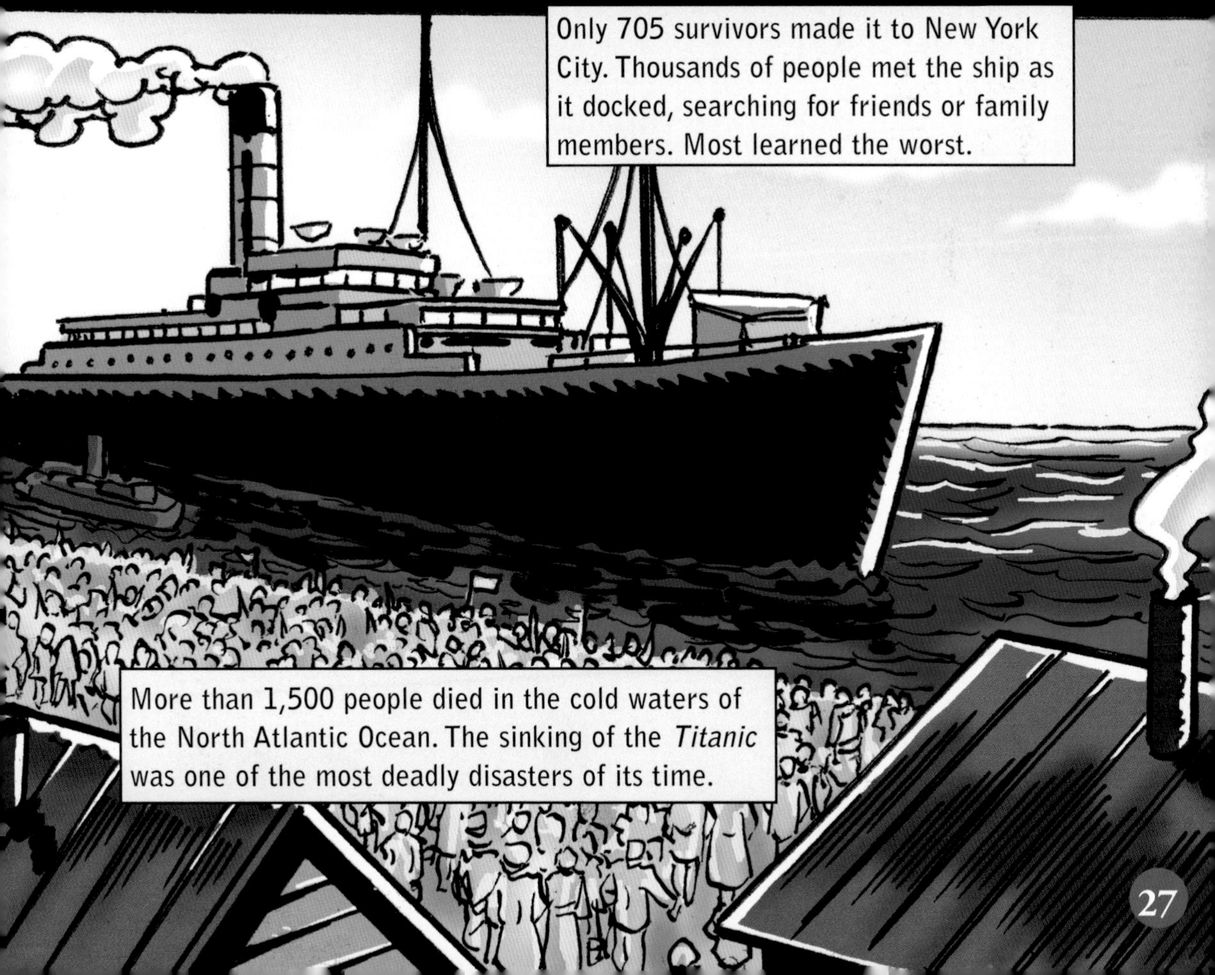
Only 705 survivors made it to New York City. Thousands of people met the ship as it docked, searching for friends or family members. Most learned the worst.
More than 1,500 people died in the cold waters of the North Atlantic Ocean. The sinking of the *Titanic* was one of the most deadly disasters of its time.

MORE ABOUT THE *TITANIC*

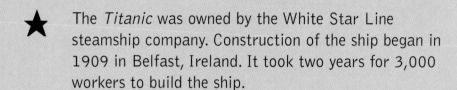

★ The *Titanic* was owned by the White Star Line steamship company. Construction of the ship began in 1909 in Belfast, Ireland. It took two years for 3,000 workers to build the ship.

★ Fully loaded, the *Titanic* weighed more than 50,000 tonnes.

★ The *Titanic* cost about £1.5 million to build. Today, it would cost about £85 million.

★ A first-class ticket on the *Titanic* cost more than a hundred times the price of a third-class ticket.

★ The *Titanic*'s first and last voyage began on 10 April 1912. After hitting the iceberg at around 11.40 at night on 14 April, the *Titanic* sank at around 2.20 in the morning on 15 April.

★ Due to a last-minute crew change, no one noticed that the binoculars were missing from the crow's nest. Some people believe that if Frederick Fleet had used binoculars, the *Titanic* could have steered clear of the iceberg. Others believe the low quality of the binoculars would not have helped Fleet see the iceberg any sooner.

★ When the *Titanic* hit the iceberg, it scraped along an underwater section of ice. The iceberg ripped many holes along a 91-metre (300-foot) section on the bottom of the ship.

★ The *Titanic* carried 20 lifeboats. To save all the passengers and crew on board, the *Titanic* would have needed 48 lifeboats.

★ The exact location of the *Titanic*'s wreckage was unknown for 73 years. Then, in 1985, Dr Robert Ballard led a team of explorers to find the *Titanic*. The team finally found the great sunken ship 4 kilometres (2.5 miles) beneath the surface of the North Atlantic Ocean.

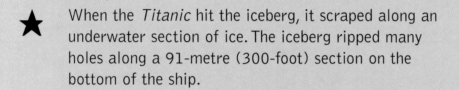

GLOSSARY

bridge control centre of a ship

crow's nest lookout post located high above the ship

distress signal call for help from a ship. Operators sent distress signals from the wireless room.

harbour place where ships load and unload passengers and cargo

hull frame or body of a ship

propeller set of rotating blades that provides the force to move a ship through water

starboard right-hand side of a ship

stern back half of a ship

INTERNET SITES

http://www.nationalarchives.gov.uk/education/lessons/lesson33.htm

This website will help you learn about the kinds of people who travelled on the *Titanic*.

http://www.bbc.co.uk/southampton/features/titanic/

On this website, you can take a tour of Southampton as it was in 1912, when the *Titanic* set sail from its harbour.

http://www.nmm.ac.uk/explore/sea-and-ships/facts/ships-and-seafarers/the-titanic

Find out some interesting facts about why the *Titanic* was built, and how it sank.

READ MORE

Eyewitness: Titanic, Simon Adams (Dorling Kindersley, 2009)

Titanic, Martin Jenkins (Walker, 2008)

When Disaster Struck: The Titanic 1912, Vic Parker (Raintree, 2007)

BIBLIOGRAPHY

The Discovery of the Titanic, Robert D. Ballard (Warner, 1987)

The History of the White Star Line, Robin Gardiner (Ian Allan, 2001)

Ice Warning Messages, The Marconi Corporation, http://www.marconicalling.com

Titanic Inquiry Project, American and British Inquiry Transcripts, http://www.titanicinquiry.com

A Night to Remember, Walter Lord (Holt, Rinehart, & Winston, 1976)

Titanic: Legacy of the World's Greatest Ocean Liner, Susan Wels (Time-Life Books, 1997)

INDEX